THE PRESIDENTIAL CAMPAIGN OF 1832

THE PRESIDENTIAL CAMPAIGN OF 1832

BY

SAMUEL RHEA GAMMON, JR., PH.D.

Professor of History in Austin College

GREENWOOD PRESS, PUBLISHERS
WESTPORT, CONNECTICUT

Originally published as Series XL No. 1 of
*Johns Hopkins University Studies in Historical and Political
Science* in 1922 by The Johns Hopkins Press, Baltimore

First Greenwood Reprinting 1971

Library of Congress Catalogue Card Number 79-114532

SBN 8371-4827-8

Printed in the United States of America

CONTENTS

PREFACE

An account of the presidential campaign of 1832, it may be well to state, cannot be confined solely to that presidential year, as might perhaps be done with a present day national campaign. Today our sharply differentiated, permanently organized parties have a definite political machinery which functions rapidly and efficiently in designating their candidates and in stating the platforms upon which they will go before the country. Consequently our national campaigns now are limited wholly to the presidential year, one might almost say to the time embraced between April and November of that year. This speed and precision of operation is due largely to our superior means of travel and communication.

Presidential campaigns during the period 1824–1832 were facilitated by no such present-day means as railroads, telegraphs, telephones, good roads and automobiles. Then, the circulation of both individual and information was limited by such speed as could be extracted from equine motive power traveling over roads which often hardly merited the name. This state of affairs the river steamboat did little to improve owing to its limited application. For this, if for no other reason, presidential campaigns were of much longer duration then than now. In addition, it was a period of political change; new parties were developing, party principles were becoming fixed, and new methods of choosing candidates were being tried. All these causes operated to make the presidential campaign of the period an affair of never less than two years' duration. That such was the case is shown by the fact that the campaign of 1824 was well under way before the close of 1822, that of 1828 began as soon as its predecessor closed, and the opening of that of 1832, by no stretch of imagination, can be put later than July 4, 1830, the date Clay's campaign for the presidency was launched.

For these reasons then, any adequate treatment of the campaign of 1832 necessitates considerable attention to much that occurred in the four years following Jackson's first election in November, 1828.

In this monograph the writer's aim has been to show the party development and the maneuvers which affected the course and outcome of the presidential campaign of 1832, and in this movement appears the first application of the nominating convention to political practice. So much has been written on the Jacksonian period that a new study requires justification, but the topics here emphasized have never been adequately treated.

So closely are the presidential campaigns of 1824, 1828 and 1832 connected by the two topics, the development of political parties and the early application of the nominating convention idea, that adequate treatment of the campaign of 1832 involves a study of the two immediately preceding it. It was this which makes necessary the brief summary of the campaigns of 1824 and 1828 contained in the first chapter. In this chapter and elsewhere I have pointed out, I believe for the first time, the significance of the first state nominating convention in Pennsylvania, the germ and precedent for its successor, the national nominating convention, and that the idea of the latter had been suggested as early as February, 1822. I have shown how Antimasonry came to inaugurate in American politics the use of the nominating convention. It has never before been clearly shown how entirely a one-man party the National Republican was in the campaign of 1832, and how hard pressed it was for a leading issue on which to oppose Jackson. I have endeavored to set forth in some detail the internal struggle for the succession in the Democratic party and the bearing of the resulting breach between Jackson and Calhoun on the campaign. In the same connection I have tried to correct the view that the Democratic convention of 1832 owed its origin solely to Jackson's determination to force Van Buren on the party as vice president. What actually took place in the three national conventions—aside from the bare references to the nominees and the two-thirds rule—regarding their establishment of precedents, such as the unit rule, which are in use today, is a neglected subject on which I have tried to throw light. Some new light has also been thrown on the political tactics of the United States Bank. Further research has brought out clearly the political paradox of 1832, a situation where Antimasons and National Republicans were both doing their utmost against Jackson yet were unable to unite behind one candidate, though both parties were well aware that certain defeat awaited their failure to combine. I have also established as nearly as possible the way in which the party names " National Republican," " Democratic " and " Democratic Republican " were used during the campaigns of 1824, 1828 and 1832, and their status at the close of the latter contest. This topic has been placed in the appendix, as it suited the structure of the monograph better there than if attached to either the chapter on the Democrats or that on the National Republicans.

This study was undertaken at the suggestion of Professor John H. Latané, of the Johns Hopkins University, to whom, with Professor John M. Vincent, also of the Johns Hopkins University, I wish to express my sincere appreciation and hearty thanks for their helpful interest and advice. To Professor J. S. Bassett, of Smith College, I am also indebted for valuable suggestions. I desire to make special acknowledgment of the unfailing kindness and courtesy of those in the Manuscript Division of the Library of Congress, and particularly of the valuable assistance rendered me by the Assistant-Chief, Mr. John C. Fitzpatrick, whose kindness in lending me the proof sheets of Van Buren's Autobiography prior to its publication so appreciably facilitated my work. Acknowledgment is also due to Mr. Charles Fickus, of the Maryland Historical Society Library, for his help in locating some useful Antimasonic pamphlets and periodicals.

S. R. G.

THE PRESIDENTIAL CAMPAIGN OF 1832

CHAPTER I

PARTY REORGANIZATION, 1824–1828

James Monroe's second administration terminated the line
of Revolutionary founders of the United States which had
filled the presidency since the inception of that office. It
likewise terminated the so-called "Virginia dynasty" which
had uninterruptedly supplied the presidential material during
the last twenty-four years. These two circumstances made
possible the complete disintegration of the old Republican
party which had come into power with the "Virginia dynasty" and was now to make a simultaneous exit.

The prime factor in the Republican party's long domination of national politics under direction of the Virginia line
of presidents was the Virginia-New York alliance. This
combination had been founded by Jefferson and indoctri-
nated with his political philosophy. Its power rested upon
the political alliance of Virginia and New York, supported
by certain States greatly under the influence of their example; namely, New Jersey in the North, and Kentucky,
North Carolina, Tennessee and Georgia in the South. Under
this combination, to Virginia went the presidential and to
New York went the vice-presidential selection. The President's influence and preference exercised such weight in the
designation of his successor that, immediately the latter was
known, he was styled by his enemies "the heir apparent." [1]

[1] Channing, History of the United States, 1789–1815, vol. iv,
chap. vi; Bassett, Life of Andrew Jackson, vol. i, pp. 323–324; cf.
Henry Adams, History of the United States, 1801–1807, vol. ii, pp.
201–206.

Just prior to the opening of the campaign of 1824, the mainsprings of the Virginia-New York alliance were two organizations known as the Richmond Junto of Virginia and the Albany Regency of New York. Each of these political organizations dominated the politics of its particular State, and hence of the adjoining States in so far as the latter inclined to follow the political lead of Virginia or New York in a presidential contest. The Junto was the looser organization of the two, being composed of some dozen men of high character, political intelligence and prominent families, with no one individual predominating. The Junto's mouthpiece was the Richmond Enquirer, whose editor, Thomas Ritchie, was one of the members. The Regency had been born in the factional struggles of New York State politics between the followers of DeWitt Clinton and Martin Van Buren. By 1822 the latter faction under Van Buren's able leadership was completely victorious, and their leader the political master of the State. The Albany Regency was a consequence of this victory and comprised the faction's leaders in the State, all upright, able men, most of whom held office of some sort at Albany. Its mouthpiece was the Albany Argus, edited by one of its members, Edwin Croswell. So effective was this machine's centralized control that, excepting about two years, it dominated the State, and was a prominent factor in national politics for over twenty years.[2]

The Republican party's character had changed markedly during the quarter century in which it had dominated the country's politics. Its rival, the Federalist party, had died, attainted with disloyalty to the country in the War of 1812, so that since 1816 it had been unopposed by any political enemy, and had come to embrace a vast majority of the entire electorate. The disappearance of political opposition

---

[2] Lynchburg Virginian, quoted in Richmond Enquirer, May 6, 1823; cf. Niles' Weekly Register, vol. xxvii, pp. 1-5, 17-21; for Regency, Thurlow Weed, Autobiography, p. 103; Jabez D. Hammond, History of Political Parties in New York, vol. ii, p. 157.

and the country's war-born tendency toward nationalism had been chiefly responsible for the change in the party's original character. The alteration had been furthered by Monroe's policy of appointing men to office with slight attention to their former political creed, and likewise by his inclination to favor internal improvements at national expense. Consequently, by 1822 the line of demarcation between a Republican and a member of the former Federalist party was so dim as to be practically invisible, and the old party landmarks had so far vanished that the Republican party was sponsor for the Bank of the United States, the protective tariff, and was markedly inclining toward a centralized nationalistic policy relative to internal improvements.[3]

The presidential campaign of 1824 was, therefore, an intraparty contest in which all the candidates, broadly speaking, professed the same principles. Consequently the contest was fought primarily on the basis of the relative personal fitness of the candidates for the presidency—a campaign of opposing persons rather than principles, the latter being subordinated to the man and used principally as incidental to his election. Hence the contest necessarily hinged on the method by which the candidate was to be nominated or selected—and therefore elected. The struggle for the coveted office was the immediate factor which shattered the Republican party into five fairly distinct factions.

Monroe was hardly well under way with his second administration before mention was being made of various individuals to succeed him. Indeed, as early as April, 1822, there were sixteen or seventeen such would-be candidates before the public.[4] This number before the end of the year had narrowed to Henry Clay, John C. Calhoun, William H.

---

[3] Van Buren, Autobiography (John C. Fitzpatrick, Ed.), Annual Report of the American Historical Association for the year 1918, vol. ii, p. 124; Niles' Register, vol. xxiii, p. 401; Richardson, Messages and Papers of the Presidents, vol. ii, pp. 144–183; James Parton, Life of Andrew Jackson, vol. iii, pp. 86–87.

[4] Niles' Register, vol. xxii, p. 130.

Crawford, John Quincy Adams and Andrew Jackson. Each of these had entered the field from a different angle and looked with more or less confidence to various sources of support for success.

Clay's course for several years had been shaped toward the presidency. Popular in the West, one of the " war hawks," negotiator at Ghent, several times Speaker of the House, he relied on this record, but more particularly on his advocacy of a high protective tariff and the construction of roads and canals at national expense—the " American System "—and of increase in the military establishment to secure him general support, especially in commercial and manufacturing New York, Pennsylvania and New England.[5] Calhoun, like Clay, relied on vigorous support of a nationalistic program, the Bank and tariff particularly, and upon his able administration of the War Department in Monroe's cabinet, together with his popularity in South Carolina and Pennsylvania.[6] Adams, favorite son of New England, negotiator at Ghent, generally admired for his skillful handling of the Department of State, a vigorous nationalist, had also in his favor the feeling that the North was now entitled to fill the presidential chair.[7]

Crawford had been near supplanting Monroe for the nomination in 1816, had been several years Secretary of the Treasury, an office controlling a great deal of patronage, and in addition was favored by Jefferson and the Virginia influence. He further had the support of a large part of the administration press. He professed Republican principles more strictly Jeffersonian as to States' Rights and internal improvements than did Clay, Calhoun or Adams. More effective still, his cause was the cause of the Regency and the

    [5] Van Buren, Autobiography, p. 116; Thomas H. Benton, Thirty Years' View, vol. i, pp. 22, 32.
    [6] Van Buren, ibid.; Hammond, vol. ii, p. 126; Gaillard Hunt, John C. Calhoun, p. 48.
    [7] Hammond, vol. ii, pp. 127–128; Parton, vol. ii, pp. 655–656; Niles' Register, vol. xxv, pp. 340, 360, 370.

Junto, and Van Buren, his chief manager, was untiring in his behalf, making several trips to Virginia to coordinate the efforts of the alliance and to confer with Jefferson and other leaders of the party.[8] Jackson's chances rested on the general admiration of his military record, the almost idolatrous worship in which he was held by the democracy of the country, especially in the West. His views on both tariff and internal improvements were not definitely known, but as far as could be ascertained from his expressions and votes in Congress, he favored both so far as they contributed to the country's military strength, and no farther.[9]

Judging by the views of these candidates on the subject of internal improvements at national expense, and by the expressions of contemporary political leaders, by the middle of 1823 there was a barely visible tendency in the Republican party to divide into two general groups on opposite sides of the question of a national, as opposed to a States' Rights, policy concerning internal improvements. Inclined, but not positively committed, to the strict construction attitude were Crawford and Jackson with their followings, so far at least as the latter heeded the constitutional side of the question. Strongly advocating the loose construction view of the national government's powers on this score were Adams, Clay and Calhoun, with their supporters. The tendency was noticed by Jefferson, Van Buren and Benton, the latter stating it thus:

The candidates for the Presidency spread their sails upon the ocean of internal improvements. Congress was full of projects for different objects of improvement, and the friends of each candidate exerted themselves in rivalry of each other, under the supposition that their opinions would stand for those of their principals. Mr.

[8] Jefferson, Writings (P. L. Ford, Ed.), vol. x, pp. 235–236; Van Buren to G. A. Worth, March 16, 1822, M. Ulshoeffer to Van Buren, April 2, 1822, Van Buren to Smith Thompson, June 4, 1823, Van Buren, MSS.; Van Buren, Autobiography, pp. 131, 177, 514.

[9] Van Buren, Autobiography, p. 449; Annals of Congress, 18th Cong., 1st sess., vol. i, pp. 583–738, passim; Bassett, Life of Andrew Jackson, vol. i, pp. 344–345; Jackson to Coleman, April 26, 1824, in Niles' Register, vol. xxvi, p. 245.

Adams, Mr. Clay, and Mr. Calhoun were the avowed advocates of
the measure, going thoroughly for a national system of internal improvements; Mr. Crawford and General Jackson under limitations
and qualifications.[10]

The number of candidates made it certain that if all remained contenders for the office none would have a majority
of the electoral votes, and the election would end in the
House of Representatives. This was universally regarded
as a very undesirable termination, but there agreement ended.
The congressional caucus, the mode of selecting the party's
candidate in use for twenty years past, pleased nobody except the Crawford faction. It was this need for some better
method than the caucus for fixing upon a candidate that produced the first suggestions that a national nominating convention of the party should be resorted to. The first of these
was in an anonymous letter to Hezekiah Niles in February,
1822;[11] Thomas Ritchie made another like suggestion in his
paper of August 13, 1822;[12] and a third was made by a member of the Pennsylvania delegation in Congress in a letter
to the editor of the Franklin Gazette dated January 6, 1824.[13]
The idea was not adopted, however, primarily it would seem,
because the divisions in the electorate caused by the several
factions prevented the general party cooperation necessary
to the establishment of this large piece of political machinery.

Under the leadership of Van Buren, who was in close con-
tact with the Junto and the older Republican leaders in Virginia, the Virginia-New York alliance backed Crawford's
candidacy, and by the summer of 1823 his chances were of
the best. At this juncture he was prostrated by a paralytic
stroke and for a time his life was despaired of. This necessarily damaged his chances with the country, but the Junto-
Regency combination would not withdraw him. Seeking to
place upon him the stamp of " regular " candidate, they began

---

[10] Benton, Thirty Years' View, vol. i, p. 22; cf. Van Buren, Autobiography, p. 116; Jefferson, Writings, vol. x, p. 282.
[11] Niles' Register, vol. xxi, pp. 403–404.
[12] Richmond Enquirer, August 13, 1822.
[13] Niles' Register, vol. xxv, p. 306.

moves looking to the holding of a congressional caucus for that purpose.

No congressional caucus had been held since that of 1816, and this one had aroused considerable adverse criticism. The functioning of such a caucus consistently with party harmony was possible only when a majority of Republican sentiment favored one candidate, a condition emphatically not the case in the pending campaign. Hence the Crawford faction's move for such a caucus savored so strongly of an attempt to force him upon the party as to bring on a revolt against the old method, in which all the other factions participated. Nevertheless the Crawford managers persisted and called a congressional caucus in February, 1824. This was so far from having present a majority of the members of Congress as to merit the name " rump." [14] Its nomination of Crawford and Gallatin injured the former's chances much more than it benefited them.[15]

The anti-caucus revolt had really been born in the democratic West with the nominations of Jackson and Clay by caucuses of their respective state legislatures in the latter part of 1822. These nominations had been endorsed by other state legislatures, using the same mode, in various Western and Southwestern States. All of these state nominations were designed to anticipate any move by the congressional caucus, and this means of forestalling its action was also adopted by the supporters of Adams and Calhoun in the East.

Jackson, more than any other candidate, was a man of the masses, hence his chief strength lay with the democratic West and Southwest. When first announced, his candidacy was not regarded seriously,[16] but this view underwent a

---

[14] Ibid., pp. 388–392, 401–406.
[15] Jackson to Donelson, February 12, 1824, A. J. Donelson MSS.; Daniel Webster, Private Correspondence (Fletcher Webster, Ed.), vol. i, p. 346.
[16] Van Buren to G. C. Verplanck, December 22, 1822, Van Buren MSS.; Richmond Enquirer, July 30, 1822.

rapid revision during 1823. During the closing months of this year Jackson sentiment spread like wildfire through the State of Pennsylvania.[17] This enthusiastic adoption of Jackson by Pennsylvania had several highly important results. It made Jackson the leading candidate by fortifying his western and southwestern strength with the twenty-eight electoral votes of Pennsylvania, a position he retained until the election entered the House of Representatives. It annihilated Calhoun's presidential candidacy, thereby causing him to withdraw in Jackson's favor in return for the latter's support of him for vice-president,[18] thus breaking ground for the future alliance of South and West. Lastly, the Pennsylvania stampede to Jackson introduced the genuine nominating convention, on a state scale, into American national politics.

This convention was in all respects the germ of the present-day national nominating convention. The call for it was issued by a caucus of the Jacksonians in the state legislature and representation in it was apportioned according to the electoral strength of the constituent units, the counties. In its organization it resorted to the plural number of vice-presidents for honorary purposes, and conducted business, in part at least, by the committee system. It made presidential nominations, chose a ticket of electors and issued an address to the people, the precedent for the modern platform.[19]

For all the desperate efforts of the Regency and Junto in behalf of Crawford, his prospects remained gloomy, and this gloom was accentuated by a complete overturn by the Clintonians in New York of the Regency's control of the State.[20]

---

[17] Niles' Register, vol. xxv, pp. 167, 194, 242, 258.

[18] Nathan Sargent, Public Men and Events, vol. i, p. 41; Niles' Register, vol. xxv, pp. 258, 407–408; vol. xxvi, pp. 19–20; Van Buren to B. F. Butler, February 2, 1824, Van Buren MSS.

[19] Niles' Register, vol. xxvi, pp. 19–20.

[20] Van Buren, Autobiography, pp. 142, 145, 149; Hammond, vol. ii, pp. 122, 131–132, 163, 165, 175–178, 188; Weed, Autobiography, pp. 107–116.

This caused the Georgian the loss of nearly all that State's thirty-six electoral votes and brought him into the House of Representatives, ahead of Clay it is true, but hopelessly behind Jackson and Adams, the respective electoral vote being for Jackson 99, Adams 84, Crawford 41 and Clay 37.[21] Thanks to the support of both the Adams and the Jackson following,[22] Calhoun was elected vice-president by a large majority of the electoral vote.

The election of John Quincy Adams by the House of Representatives was directly due to the influence and personal efforts of Henry Clay.[23] The Kentuckian's assistance had been courted by both Adams and Jackson men. Hence the charge that his support of Adams had been secured by means of a promise of the State Department, and originating with one of the Jacksonians, is not surprising, the less so, in fact, since the campaign just ended had been mainly one of personalities and recriminations. Although the charge against Clay was not proven, its falsity was never conclusively demonstrated; but true or false, it was destined to play a prominent part in shaping party combinations.

Among the results of the campaign, the first to be accomplished was the complete obliteration of the already faint line between the former Federalist and Republican parties. The most potent factor in this had been Jackson's candidacy, coming as it did on the heels of Monroe's amalgamation policy. The Tennessean's large popular vote and electoral plurality were due to the general admiration of his military record and to a widespread conviction of his integrity and sincerity. To these was added also the widespread aversion to the caucus system.[24] Furthermore, some letters that Jackson himself had written to Monroe some eight years

---

[21] Van Buren, Autobiography, pp. 144–145; Hammond, vol. ii, pp. 177, 178, 188; Niles' Register, vol. xxvii, p. 382.

[22] Niles' Register, vol. xxvii, p. 382

[23] Van Buren, Autobiography, pp. 149–153; Hammond, vol. ii, p. 189.

[24] Van Buren, Autobiography, p. 449.

earlier had been used in the campaign. These contained an appeal to Monroe to exterminate the monster of party spirit by appointing to office men of ability and integrity regardless of their former party affiliation.[25] These letters must have been of considerable effect in drawing to Jackson the support of former Federalists, for so many of them supported him that, according to Van Buren, the vote he received was "a mixed one given by former adherents of all parties."[26]

Another result of the campaign, produced by the movement toward popular nominations, had been the complete demolition of the congressional caucus as a means of nominating presidential candidates. This old method had been replaced by the individual state nominations made by party caucuses in the legislatures. This substitute was effective, but far too prone to militate against the unity and discipline of an organized party to remain other than a temporary expedient. Suggestions for a national nominating convention had been made, however, and the state nominating convention in Pennsylvania had established a precedent admirably adapted to a democracy, based as it was upon popular representation apportioned according to electoral strength. The disappearance of the caucus, furthermore, transferred the seat of president-making, that is, the selecting of the party candidates, from a relative handful of individuals in Washington, to the country at large; hence in future campaigns every cross-roads, hamlet, village and town would be able to participate actively.

A third result of the campaign was the dissolution of the Virginia-New York alliance. Only Georgia, among the four States formerly dominated by Virginia, had remained loyal to Crawford, the remainder being distributed between Jackson, Adams and Clay. New Jersey had broken away from New York's leading, and the latter State had over-

---

[25] Jackson to Monroe, October 23, November 12, 1816, January 6, 1817, Jackson MSS.
[26] Van Buren, Autobiography, p. 449.

thrown the Regency's control. This failure of the Regency had been the prime, if not the sole, cause of Crawford's crushing defeat, and since failure is one of the deadliest sins a political machine can commit, it is not surprising that relations between Junto and Regency for a time totally ceased.[27]

The most important single result of the campaign was the shattering into five factions of the old Republican party. A corollary of this, but equally important, was the tendency, faintly visible as early as 1823, of these five factions to coalesce into two groups—the one very mildly in favor of, the other wholly committed to, a nationalistic program. The leaders of the first were Crawford and Jackson, of the second, Clay, Adams and Calhoun.[28]

Clay's acceptance of the State Department from Adams entailed results more far-reaching than are perceptible at first glance. It cemented indissolubly the political fortunes of the two men, and was immediately responsible for the merging of their respective factions, readily possible from their entire accord as to a nationalistic policy founded on loose construction. Clay's acceptance lent color to the "corrupt bargain" charge, laid against him by the Jacksonians, of obtaining his office in return for supporting Adams' election in the House of Representatives. This charge was at once circulated all over the country and kept resounding for the next four years. This with the other furious attacks on the new administration rendered it impossible for Clay to withdraw from his position even had he desired.

The least known of the consequences of Clay's union with Adams was its effect on Calhoun. The latter, elected vice-president by virtue of the support of both Adams' and Jackson's followers, was in a position to incline his political strength toward either of them. His course seems to have been dictated purely by self-interest. As soon as he learned

---

[27] Philip N. Nicholas to Van Buren, October 13, 1826, Van Buren MSS.

[28] Cf. Benton, Thirty Years' View, vol. i, p. 22; Van Buren, Autobiography, p. 116; Jefferson, Writings, vol. x, p. 282.

of Adams' intention to appoint Clay Secretary of State, and therefore his probable successor, Calhoun made it known to the President that in this event he would join the opposition and assist in organizing it behind Jackson; he even went so far as to suggest what men he preferred in the new cabinet.[29] Adams ignored this threat and Calhoun within the year turned to the Jacksonians.

The simultaneous wreck of Crawford's health and presidential aspirations resulted in his withdrawal from national politics. His followers, who regarded themselves and were generally considered doctrinally as the true Republicans of the old school among the adherents of the late Virginia-New York alliance, remained aloof from initial attacks on Adams and Clay. Badly disorganized, they were now confronted with the problem of choosing a new political chief. Jackson's indefinite constitutional views and uncertain attitude toward internal improvements caused them some hesitation in joining him; but between his uncertainty and the nationalist tendencies of the Adams-Clay group they naturally preferred the former.

Adams' inaugural address and his first annual message to Congress, particularly the latter, gave all loose constructionists a wholly gratuitous shove Jacksonward. Its phrase as to the folly of being " palsied by the will of our constituents "[30] in the vigorous prosecution of a centralized nationalistic program, was the signal for a furious outburst of denunciation from the Jackson, Crawford and Calhoun press. Following his inaugural address, which had been in tone a forecast of his first annual message, the confirmation of Clay's nomination had been attacked in the Senate by the Jacksonians, supported by a few Crawford and Calhoun senators.[31]   In

[29] John Quincy Adams, Memoirs (C. F. Adams, Ed.), vol. vi, p. 507.
[30] Richardson, Messages and Papers, vol. ii, pp. 311–317. The phrase quoted above occurred in his first annual message to Congress.
[31] Niles' Register, vol. xxviii, p. 17; Benton, Thirty Years' View, vol. i, p. 55.

the following April John Marshall wrote Clay from Richmond that there were signs of a violent opposition to the administration forming.[32]   In June Van Buren openly came out in favor of Jackson for next president.[33]   In short, the former Calhoun and Crawford men were gravitating rapidly toward Jackson, and this gain more than counterbalanced any losses resulting from the defection of his Federalist following to Adams.   Hence the President's first annual message was tantamount to driving home a nail already started.   It now only remained to clinch it; namely, to unite firmly behind Jackson the Regency-Junto combination in New York and Virginia.

In Congress the opposition to the administration rapidly solidified.   Van Buren and Calhoun conferred and agreed in attacking the President's proposed Panama Mission.   Van Buren led the fight on the Senate floor, ably seconded by Randolph, by Hayne of South Carolina and by Benton of Missouri.   The attacks were by no means limited to this subject alone, but embraced every conceivable means of harassing or discrediting the policy of the administration before the country.

As a result of the war upon the executive in and out of Congress, by the time that body adjourned in May, 1826, the lines, both party and constitutional, upon which the next campaign was to be fought were clearly drawn.   It would be Adams or Jackson; a nationalistic governmental policy, or the rule of the masses and reform.   The campaign was to be based, however, more upon the personality of the candidates than upon the principles which they represented.   In a contest of this kind all the advantage would be with Jackson.   Adams, though a statesman, trained administrator and diplomatist, was totally lacking in the personal qualities that make up a leader.   He was much too stiff, too cold and

[32] John Marshall to Clay, April 4, 1825, Clay, Private Correspondence (Colton, Ed.), p. 121.

[33] Van Buren, Autobiography, pp. 198–199.

austere, to arouse popular enthusiasm or to attract a large personal following. Jackson was everything Adams was not in this respect. His picturesque career, combativeness, devotion to friends and fiery courage had made him the idol of the West, the more so since that section as a whole was convinced that his defeat in the House of Representatives had been due to political trickery and to a disregard of the popular will.[34] Furthermore, since the abolition of the congressional caucus, nominations and president-making could no longer be exclusively manipulated from Washington, and this gave Jackson's democratic following much more weight than it had possessed in the late campaign.

Jackson's campaign was carefully organized and ably conducted. Composing his support were three distinct elements or wings: the followers of Calhoun, principally in Pennsylvania, the Carolinas and Alabama; the former Crawford strength, chiefly in New York, Virginia and Georgia; Jackson's own democratic following in the West and in Pennsylvania. The Calhoun wing of the party was dominant at Washington. It was led by Calhoun himself, supported by a number of other prominent men of national reputation, and though numerically the weakest section of Jackson's support, in personal influence it was the strongest. It also controlled the party organ, the United States Telegraph,[35] whose editor, Duff Green, was father-in-law of Calhoun's son. Next to the Calhoun group in the prominence of its leaders was the Crawford wing, led by Van Buren. This group, provided the Regency could regain control of New York and reestablish the alliance with the Junto, would be decidedly stronger numerically than that of Calhoun; but aside from Van Buren, it possessed no man of the caliber of Hayne, Cheves, Dallas, McDuffie and others in Calhoun's train. In Van Buren, however, it had a leader without a peer in the

---

[34] Undated paper in John McLean's handwriting, apparently written about 1828, in McLean MSS.

[35] Van Buren, Autobiography, pp. 514–515.

country for political acumen, judgment and management. Strongest in numbers, Jackson's western and Pennsylvania supporters formed the basis of his strength, but they were weak in leaders of national importance. Such men as Hugh L. White, John H. Eaton, Kendall and Hill were numerous among them, but of leaders of the Calhoun type as to reputation, prominence and culture, they had few, and none at all comparable to Van Buren as a political manager and organizer.

It had been made painfully clear to the Jacksonians, that to achieve success against an opponent who, like Adams, could rely upon the solid 51 electoral votes of New England, at least two of the three largest States—New York, Pennsylvania and Virginia—were necessary to their candidate in addition to his southern and western support. Upon Pennsylvania they could rely, but the vote of New York and Virginia was another matter. In Virginia prejudice against an administration headed by Jackson, and therefore redolent of the masses, was hardly less strong than the dislike of Adams' latitudinarianism.[36] In New York, Jackson had had little or no support in 1824, hence it is apparent how essential to his cause was the reestablishment of the Regency's control of New York under Van Buren and a renewal of the entente between it and the Junto in Virginia.

The achievement of this constituted Van Buren's most vital service to the Jacksonian cause. By adroit handling he and the Regency not only regained political control of New York through reducing Clinton's support to a bare majority in the state election in 1826, but they also successfully alienated him from Adams and Clay and secured his not wholly enthusiastic adherence to Jackson.[37] By apparently doing no more than allowing the Richmond Junto to realize the rather unpalatable alternative of choosing between Adams'

[36] Nicholas to Van Buren, October 13, 1826, Van Buren MSS.
[37] Niles' Register, vol. xxxi, pp. 178, 210, 242; Van Buren, Autobiography, pp. 158-165; Hammond, vol. ii, pp. 207, 232-235, 256-257.

uncompromising nationalistic proclivities and the rule of the western democracy through Jackson, Van Buren, by October, 1826, found the Junto again ready to join forces with the Regency in supporting Jackson.[38]   He therefore lost no time in welcoming this accession to the party's strength, and thus under his leadership the New York-Virginia alliance was restored.[39]   Unlike its combination, broken in 1824, New York was now the senior partner, and the alliance's political strength was now limited mainly to the two States.

Van Buren's services to the Jackson party did not end with reforming the New York-Virginia alliance.   He worked hard to harmonize the Crawford and Calhoun wings of the party in the East from New York to Georgia.   Immediately after restoring cooperation between Regency and Junto, accompanied by his lieutenant Cambreleng, he traveled from New York to Georgia through Virginia and the Carolinas, stopping for some days with James Hamilton and other Calhoun leaders in Charleston, and visiting his former chief, Crawford, in Georgia.[40]   In addition to this, he corresponded with Calhoun and Jackson leaders in Pennsylvania,[41] and cooperated in harmony with Calhoun in Washington during the sessions of Congress.[42]

From the termination of the congressional elections of 1826–1827, in which the Jacksonians everywhere made large gains, until the presidential election, the campaign raged with a fury unprecedented in American politics.   In its course principles were entirely subordinated to personalities, and in this respect it far outstripped the campaign of 1824, in which the abuse and recrimination had at least been distributed among several candidates.   Now the struggle was

---

[38] Nicholas to Van Buren, October 13, 1826, Van Buren MSS.
[39] Undated letter in Van Buren's hand in reply to that of Nicholas; Van Buren to Ritchie, January 13, 1827, Van Buren MSS.; Clay to Brook, December 23, 1826, Clay, Correspondence, p. 153.
[40] Van Buren, Autobiography, pp. 169, 367; Niles' Register, vol. xxxii, p. 198.
[41] Ingham to Van Buren, September 26, 1828, Van Buren MSS.
[42] Van Buren, Autobiography, pp. 200–202, 514–517.

limited to two, with the entire nation supporting one or the other, and the dominating principle was, anything to beat Jackson or Adams as the case might be—a question of the superior fitness of the person to be selected rather than of the political principles. One of the candidates was seeking re-election to office, an office which, according to his enemies, he held by virtue of a political bargain and sale; the other was possessed of a highly spectacular past. With such sources from which to draw charges and counter-charges, it is not surprising that the campaign has never been surpassed in our political history in bitterness of personal recrimination and in the extent to which it carried the villification and defamation not only of the candidates themselves, but of their families and friends as well.

In this campaign the tendency, noted above, of factions to align on opposite sides of the issue of a strongly nationalistic and centralized governmental policy, completed its initial stages. Two sharply defined political parties are plainly apparent before Adams had been in office a year. Marshall's letter to Clay, warning him that "there is unquestionably a party determined to oppose Mr. Adams at the next election," has already been noticed.[43] In January, 1826, Clay wrote Webster of his perfect confidence that Adams would be elected in spite of the opposition.[44] Later in the same year he wrote him "at this time there are but two parties in the Union, that of the administration, and the opposition."[45] In another letter a few months later, he expressed the party situation as follows: "It appears to me to be important that we should, on all occasions, inculcate the incontestable truth that *now* there are but two parties in the Union, the friends and the enemies of the administration."[46]

To the Crawford men who joined Jackson early in the campaign, and who claimed to be the true Republicans of the

[43] Marshall to Clay, April 4, 1825, Clay, Correspondence, p. 121.
[44] Clay to Webster, January 14, 1826, Webster MSS.
[45] Ibid., November 10, 1826.
[46] Ibid., April 14, 1827.

school of 1798, Jackson's attitude on the question of strict versus loose construction, while not as clear as they wished, was far preferable to the latitudinarian views of Adams. Both Albany Regency and Richmond Junto were clear on that point. It was this very vagueness, almost amounting to equivocation, in Jackson's position, which had enabled Calhoun and his followers to ally themselves with the Jacksonians in the late campaign.

As the anti-tariff agitation, beginning in 1823–1824, rose in South Carolina, Jackson's non-committal attitude enabled him to hold on to both the Pennsylvania and South Carolina elements which constituted Calhoun's strength. Not so with Calhoun. Pennsylvania, his former stronghold, remained in favor of protection. South Carolina's violent revolt against nationalism, part of which was her objection to the tariff of 1824, forced Calhoun to reverse his former nationalistic attitude. His change of heart was publicly announced on February 28, 1827, when the highly protective "woolens bill" was before the Senate and a tie vote forced him as vice-president to pass or defeat the measure.[47] His vote against it, a bill popular in Pennsylvania, weakened materially his political strength in that State and limited his following to the South. Of his former Pennsylvania supporters all but relatively few, but these including several prominent state leaders like Ingham, became staunch Jacksonians beyond Calhoun's power to shake. On the other hand Jackson's tariff views were sufficiently indefinite to hold the allegiance of the Calhoun men in the South, more especially since Adams and nationalism were the only alternatives.

In the last year of the campaign of 1828, the state convention as a means of nominating presidential tickets reached its highest development and widest use; indeed, for the most part it superseded the state legislative caucus for this pur-

---

[47] Albany Argus, March 19, 1827; Van Buren, Autobiography, p. 169.

pose, especially in the more democratic States.[48] In the use of this instrumentality, Pennsylvania again led the way. The conventions of both parties in this State met early in January, 1828, their principal object in each case being the vice-presidential nomination. Presidential candidates of course were named, but this was merely endorsing an accomplished fact.[49] The state nominating convention itself was destined to be superseded in turn in the next campaign by its logical offspring on a national scale, but continued in use to some extent for a considerably longer period. Its adoption in 1824, however, marks the first application of the true nominating convention idea, with representation based on the electoral strength of the component units, the counties.

One other event of the campaign should be noticed, the birth of Antimasonry in New York, resulting from the abduction and probable murder of William Morgan.[50] So rapidly did this party grow, that one year after Morgan's disappearance it had elected fifteen members of the state legislature,[51] and the Regency could not safely allow it to join forces with the administration's supporters in the State. There was danger that this would occur, for, while Adams was not a Mason, Jackson was high in the counsels of the order. Hence both Regency and Adams men worked to win the support of the Antimasonic party.[52] In this contest the Adams party was successful; indeed its only hope of carrying the State was by virtue of Antimasonic aid.[53]

---

[48] Niles' Register, vol. xxxiii, pp. 129, 315–316, 332–334; Richmond Enquirer, January 10, 17, 1828; United States Telegraph, January 17, 22, 30, 1828; Pennsylvania Reporter and Democratic Herald, January 6, 11, 1828.

[49] Niles' Register, vol. xxxiii, pp. 316, 332–334; National Gazette, January 10, 1828; Pennsylvania Reporter, January 11, 1828; United States Telegraph, January 17, 1828; Van Buren, Autobiography, pp. 514–516.

[50] Weed, Autobiography, p. 242; Hammond, vol. ii, pp. 378–385.

[51] Charles McCarthy, "The Antimasonic Party," in Annual Report of the American Historical Association for the Year 1902, vol. i, chap. xvi, pp. 371–374; Albany Argus, November 23, 1827.

[52] Hammond, vol. ii, p. 386.

[53] Thurlow Weed Barnes, A Memoir of Thurlow Weed, p. 32.

Had the Antimasons been solidly united in supporting the Adams convention's nominees for governor and lieutenant-governor, Thompson and Granger.[54] the latter an Antimason, the two parties together might have carried the State in spite of the Regency. A split, however, among the Antimasons led the more radical element to put a separate ticket in the field—Southwick and Crary [55]—which made success impossible. Van Buren had meanwhile been watching the situation closely, and in the summers of 1827 and 1828 had made trips through the doubtful western part of the State.[56] He assured Jackson of a decided majority of the State's vote,[57] but nevertheless deemed it advisable to head the state ticket himself, and accordingly was nominated for governor by the Regency's convention in September, 1828.[58]

Long before the presidential ballots were cast in November, 1828, observers, even those friendly to Adams, foresaw the outcome.[59]   Clay himself admitted that " it is mortifying and sickening to the hearts of the real lovers of free government that the contest should be so close, and that if heaven grants us success it will be perhaps by less than a majority of six votes." [60]   The event realized the administration's worst fears. It was a Jackson landslide. Every State in the entire South and West—Clay's own Kentucky included—gave Jackson its entire electoral vote. Excepting New Jersey and Delaware, six votes from Maryland and sixteen from New York, Jackson carried all the Middle States. Even in New England he received one vote from Maine and rolled up a large minority of the popular vote in that State and in New Hampshire. So well had Van Buren and the Regency done their work that, despite the efforts of the ad-

[54] Adams Convention held at Utica, July 23, 1828, Albany Argus, August 4, 1828; Weed, pp. 302–303.
[55] Hammond, vol. ii, p. 389.
[56] Ibid., p. 288.
[57] Van Buren to Jackson, September 14, 1827, Van Buren MSS.
[58] Niles' Register, vol. xxxiv, p. 346; Hammond, vol. ii, p. 288.
[59] Hammond, vol. ii, p. 286.
[60] Clay to Webster, October 24, 1828, Webster MSS.

ministration and the Antimasòns, twenty of New York's thirty-six votes went to Jackson, and the Junto carried Virginia by a majority of 15,000.[61]

The election had been a fight between democracy and aristocracy primarily—both terms used in their looser sense—and a struggle between particularism and centralization secondarily. Each party, in theory at least, however much in practice it resorted to personal attacks upon its opponent, advocated certain definite principles of governmental policy which it proposed to practice if successful. With the Adams-Clay men it was the "American System." With the Jacksonians it was the rule of the people, to be instituted by a reform of the corruptions and abuses alleged by them to exist in the government and to have grown out of Adams' federalism and his corrupt bargain with Clay. The Jackson party leaders of the western group, their president-elect especially, regarded the result as "a triumph of virtue and republican simplicity over corruption and an unprincipled aristocracy."[62] "The people expect reform," said Jackson, "they shall not be disappointed; but it must be *judiciously* done, and upon *principle.*"[63]

The campaign had very decided effects upon the political party situation. It eliminated Adams as head of the nationalistic republicans, which resulted in the turning of all eyes in that party toward Clay as its future leader,[64] and thus left him heir to the remnant of Adams' following. It produced the first definite political alliance between the South and the West. It saw the weakening of Calhoun as the result of his enforced adoption of his State's about-face from nationalism to particularism.[65] Most important of all, it brought about the election of Andrew Jackson. This last

---

[61] Richmond Enquirer, November 28, 1828.

[62] William B. Lewis to James A. Hamilton, December 12, 1828, Van Buren MSS.

[63] Jackson to Van Buren, March 31, 1829, Jackson MSS.

[64] The Marylander, November 19, 1828.

[65] Houston, A Critical Study of Nullification in South Carolina, pp. 60–64.

had been accomplished by no definite political party, properly speaking, but by the support of his democratic admirers west of the Alleghenies reinforced by the followers of Crawford and Calhoun in the East and South. In this loose combination leading parts had been played by Calhoun, again vice-president-elect, and a number of his adherents who were nationally prominent. Important though their services to the Jackson cause were, they had been far surpassed by those rendered by Martin Van Buren.

CHAPTER II

THE ANTIMASONS

As already mentioned, the Antimasonic party participated in its first national campaign in 1828, being then confined to the State of New York. Almost from its inception the party suffered from a divided leadership. The mass of it was almost fanatical in its attitude toward Masonry and toward anyone even remotely connected with that institution. This extreme wing of the Antimasons favored the destruction of Masonry, first and foremost, and intended, by subordinating all other political issues, to accomplish its ends through a majority in the State legislature. On the other hand the ablest and most prominent leaders, Weed, Tracy, Whittlesey, Fitch and others,[1] desired to utilize the movement for political ends primarily, and therefore did not hesitate to bend, or to sacrifice if necessary, the party's principles to expediency.[2]

For convenience we may refer to these two elements in the party as the extremists and the politicians. The former composed the bulk of the party; the latter had a monopoly in experienced political leadership. It was this condition which led most of the extremists to refuse to follow the politicians in joining forces with the Adams party in New York in the campaign of 1828, and to nominate as a separate gubernatorial ticket Southwick and Crary.[3] But for this division it is probable that Van Buren would have been defeated for governor that year, and that Jackson would have received only a minority of the State's electoral vote.[4]

---

[1] Weed, Autobiography, p. 336.
[2] McCarthy, The Antimasonic Party, p. 383.
[3] Niles' Register, vol. xxxv, p. 89.
[4] William H. Seward, Autobiography, 1801–1834 (F. H. Seward, Ed.), pp. 73–74.

The Utica convention of August 4, 1828,—the first Antimasonic state convention and that in which the politicians had tried to ally the party with the National Republicans—had appointed a general corresponding committee for the State, composed of Whittlesey, Weed, Backus, Works and Ely, all able politicians, and had empowered it to call future state conventions when it deemed necessary.[5] Two points in this connection are interesting to note. From their first local beginnings, the Antimasons resorted mainly to the small convention; hence it was natural that when their movement became statewide they should follow the precedent established by the Pennsylvania Jacksonians in 1824 and resort to the state convention, as they did at Utica in 1828. Second, this state corresponding committee of the Antimasons was exactly analogous in function to the present-day National Committee, which analogy was further exemplified when it called a state convention of its party and designated the time, the place, and the size of delegations.[6]

The convention thus called met at Albany, February 19, 1829.[7] It was highly important for two reasons. It marked the Antimasons' point of departure from state into national politics, while its proceedings and organization formed a model and precedent according to which its offspring, the national convention of Philadelphia in 1830, was operated.

After a reconciliation between the extremists and the politicians, this Albany convention adopted a resolution disavowing connection with any political party, State or national, and proposed to run an Antimasonic ticket at every subsequent state election, whether local or general.[8] Except for a resolution appointing a general central committee of correspondence for the State, composed mainly of the politicians, the other acts of the convention were of a nature to further

---

[5] Proceedings of the Albany Convention, in Antimasonic Pamphlets, Maryland Historical Society.
[6] Ibid.
[7] Albany Argus, Feb. 20, 1829.
[8] Proceedings of the Albany Convention.

the party propaganda. Despite the strong element of extremists present, the superior political and forensic ability of Weed, Whittlesey, Fitch, Granger and others of the political element enabled them to dominate the convention's activities. Only one of its acts merits closer observation. Among several propagandic resolutions, Timothy Fitch proposed one to appoint a committee of five to " enquire whether it is expedient for this convention to recommend a convention of delegates from the several United States, to be held at some future time and place, to deliberate on " the furtherance of Antimasonic principles, "and if so whether it is expedient for this convention to designate the time, and place, and also the number of delegates for each State."[9]

This motion was adopted and Granger, Seward, Robinson, Lay and Green were appointed on the committee. Some hours later Granger reported for the committee that they had found such action expedient and submitted a resolution to hold a national convention of Antimasons at Philadelphia, on the 11th of September, 1830, the delegates to be elected as each State saw fit and to equal in number its representation in Congress. The objects stated in the resolution for holding this national convention were the adoption of measures looking to the destruction of Masonry and similar secret societies. After submitting it, Granger made some explanatory remarks. He stated that the committee, in recommending this course, had been actuated by information from newspapers and private letters that conditions were ripe for a general spread of Antimasonry in most of the States north of Maryland, and hence it seemed an auspicious time in which to hold a national convention for Antimasonic purposes. The resolution was adopted and thus the machinery was set in motion which resulted in our first political party convention.[10]

Although the ultimate aim of the politicians was doubtless to enter the field of national politics, it was too early

---

[9] Ibid.; Albany Argus, Feb. 23, 1829.
[10] Ibid.

to let this be known to the party generally, hence the language of the above resolution and the remarks made when it was presented show that its authors intended to convey the idea that this national convention was to be simply a means of spreading Antimasonry, and of uniting all efforts to break up the Masonic institution. What individual first suggested this national convention is unknown. Its alleged objects being what they were, it seems highly probable that the plan was borrowed from the Masonic practice of holding General Grand Encampments made up of delegates from the state organizations, as in 1826. This idea, indeed, was mentioned by Granger as an argument for defending the proposed convention against charges of ulterior motives.[11] Henry Ward Dana's Antimasonic Review also justifies the Philadelphia convention on the same ground.[12]

Antimasonry, thus planning to enter upon a national career, was essentially anti-Jackson as well. Its extremists naturally were opposed to Jackson, who was a high Mason, and its politician element saw in him a formidable obstacle to local and national political progress. As noted above, in 1827 both the Adams and the Jackson party had made efforts to secure the Antimasonic support in New York. That this contest terminated in favor of Adams naturally set the Regency in New York and Jackson's followers elsewhere firmly against Antimasonry. During the campaign of 1828 a letter from Adams stating that he never had been and never would be a Mason [13] had helped to draw his party and the Antimasonic politician element together. The doings at Albany, and especially the personnel of the state central committee appointed by that convention, prove conclusively that the anti-Jackson politicians among the Antimasons were again leading the party. It was with this group that the resolution for a national convention at Philadelphia originated.[14]

---

[11] Proceedings of the Albany Convention, Granger's Report.
[12] Ibid.; The Antimasonic Review, I, vol. xii, p. 365.
[13] Weed. Autobiography, p. 312.
[14] The Antimasonic Review, I, vol. xii, pp. 364–365.

Between this convention at Albany and that at Philadelphia, the Antimasonic movement spread in the States of Vermont, Massachusetts, Connecticut, Rhode Island, Pennsylvania and Ohio with unprecedented rapidity.[15] The initial excitement aroused by Morgan's disappearance and probable murder was kept stirred by a series of reports, investigations and trials in New York until well into 1829.[16] This agitation was exploited and constantly fanned in the public mind by the party's frequent conventions and by the notice given by such papers as Weed's Antimasonic Enquirer and Ward's Antimasonic Review to their resolutions and addresses.[17] In this manner the charge was spread far and wide that the Masons controlled and intimidated legislatures, judges and juries, and that Masonic obligations constituted a tie upon the individual more binding than the national constitution and laws.

That the Antimasonic leaders were planning, despite the purely propagandic motives alleged by them at Albany, to utilize the Philadelphia convention as a means of entering the next presidential campaign is shown by their cautious casting about for a candidate previous to the date on which the convention was to assemble. They preferred Clay as their candidate because he had the most numerous following outside the Jackson party, but Clay himself was a Mason and it was not certain that he would renounce his allegiance to the order. Accordingly, he was sounded through his friends, and John McLean of the Supreme Court was also approached on the subject of Masonry before the Philadelphia convention met.[18] From Clay's friends came nothing definite as to his attitude toward Masonry, though they were profuse in cordiality and in assurances that Clay was the

---

[15] Ibid., James Buchanan to McLean, June 11, 1829, McLean MSS.; Niles' Register, vol. xxxvii, p. 276.
[16] Weed, Autobiography, pp. 285–299.
[17] Ibid., p. 310.
[18] Ibid., pp. 351–352; G. W. Harris to McLean, May —, 1830, McLean MSS.

only man capable of defeating Jackson.[19] McLean wrote
that he was not and never had been a Mason, but as he
knew nothing of Masonic doctrines he could neither approve
nor condemn them.[20]

Near the end of February, 1830, state conventions of
Antimasons at Albany and Harrisburg[21] selected delegates
to the Philadelphia convention. The former of these saw
the exit of the extremist faction from all participation in
the party's policy, since Southwick's paper was discarded in
favor of Weed and his newly established Albany Evening
Journal, as the state party organ.[22] This convention also
gives further evidence of the leaders' intentions to enter
national politics with vigor, and to supplant the National
Republicans as the chief opposition party.[23] It further reveals that Antimasonry had been making great progress
not only in New York but in other neighboring States.[24]

The convention of Antimasons which met at Philadelphia
on September 11, 1830, was the first party convention on a
national scale in our political history.[25] The credit for the
application of the national convention idea to the party rests
with Fitch and the committee which recommended it at
Albany, though, as has been shown, the idea was not a new
one.[26] The convention numbered 96 delegates from the ten
States of New York, Pennsylvania, Massachusetts, Connecticut, Rhode Island, Vermont, New Jersey, Delaware,
Maryland and Ohio. The party in New York was recognized as the prime mover; indeed, the entire proceedings
were controlled by that State's delegation aided by those of

---

[19] Weed, Autobiography, pp. 351–352.
[20] McLean to G. W. Harris, May 24, 1830, McLean MSS.
[21] Niles' Register, xxxviii, p. 48; Hammond, vol. ii, p. 394.
[22] Weed, Autobiography, chap. xxxii; McCarthy, The Antimasonic Party, pp. 393–394.
[23] Seward, Autobiography, p. 77.
[24] Ibid. Cf. Niles' Register, vol. xxxvii, p. 276.
[25] National Gazette [Philadelphia], September 13, 1830; T. W.
Barnes, Memoir of Thurlow Weed, p. 39.
[26] Proceedings of the Albany Convention.

Pennsylvania and Massachusetts.[27] These three with 26, 25 and 15 delegates respectively mustered about two-thirds of the total number present.[28] This control was reflected throughout the convention's proceedings. With hardly an exception every important committee was headed by a New York, a Massachusetts or a Pennsylvania man.[29] Indeed a comparison of the two shows a conspicuous likeness of the Philadelphia convention's proceedings to those at Albany eighteen months before.

The convention's organization was effected thus. On motion by Whittlesey, a chairman and secretary pro tempore, both of Pennsylvania, were elected. A roll call of delegates by States, beginning with New York, followed, but there was no examination of credentials. Whittlesey then moved that a permanent chairman, four vice-presidents and two secretaries be elected. These had been selected by caucus some hours before the meeting convened, and accordingly were now elected, Francis Granger being chosen permanent chairman. He then made a brief speech of acknowledgment and reminded the meeting of the importance of its deliberations to the party's cause. On Whittlesey's motion the president then appointed a committee of one from each State on order of business. This completed the organization.[30]

The next day Phelps of Massachusetts, chairman of the committee on business, reported fourteen separate resolutions each providing for a separate committee. The first of these was to be a committee on rules of procedure; the remainder were charged with rendering reports on different phases of Masonic obligations and the effect of the latter on activities as diverse as commerce and Christianity, and with reporting means of spreading Antimasonic propaganda. These com-

---

[27] National Gazette [Philadelphia], September 13, 1830.
[28] Proceedings of the Philadelphia Convention, in Antimasonic Pamphlets, Maryland Historical Society.
[29] Ibid.
[30] Ibid.

mittees were formed according to both the plan and the objects pursued by the Albany convention. To them was added a finance committee authorized to raise money from among the delegates, and they all reported during the week, September 13 to 17 inclusive. Their reports were all adopted without more than casual debate and were ordered printed in the proceedings.[31]

The main point around which interest centered was the question of what should be the party's next move. There was of course no objection to another national propagandic convention such as the extremist element expected this to be; but this would obviously not suit the politicians. Hence the threefold question was raised: Should this convention stamp itself as primarily a political one by nominating a presidential ticket? Should such nomination be deferred to a later season and another convention for that purpose? Or should no action at all of such nature be considered? On the one hand were the extremists who favored fighting Masonry to the death by means of intra-state organization and propaganda; on the other were the politicians, now indubitably the party leaders, who wanted a national political organization headed by a presidential ticket in 1832.

The whole question was precipitated by Curtenius, an obscure New York delegate, when on the second day of the convention he suddenly moved for a committee to report the most expedient time, place and manner of nominating a presidential ticket. It was immediately objected to as inexpedient and was tabled. Nothing more was said on the subject until the next afternoon, when Curtenius withdrew the motion. This was not what the leaders wanted, and Whittlesey, supported by Phelps, immediately renewed it. This brought on the debate in which the extremists made a last stand against the schemes of the politicians for making Antimasonry a national political party.[32]

---

[31] Proceedings of the Philadelphia Convention.
[32] Ibid.

For the extremists, Jones and Todd of Pennsylvania led the fight and insisted that Antimasonry was not strong enough or widely enough disseminated, and that the delegates were unauthorized by their constituents to take such action. On the politicians' side, Whittlesey, Phelps, Irwin and Thaddeus Stevens supported the motion vigorously. They insisted that Antimasonry to be most effective must necessarily be political, and that a presidential ticket would bring the party into wider notice. Irwin and Stevens even went to the point of advocating an immediate nomination by the convention.

Whittlesey's motion was then amended to provide that a committee of one from each State be appointed to consider and report: (1) on the expediency of the party nominating a presidential ticket before the next election, (2) "on the *manner, time,* and *place* of making such nominations." Two days later Amos Ellmaker, chairman of the committee, reported as follows: (1) That a nomination of a presidential ticket by the party was desirable, because the Masons held two-thirds of the national government offices and could be reached only by Antimasonry controlling those offices, and because such nomination would extend Antimasonry, bring it to more general notice and pave the way to success in 1836 if not in 1832; (2) That they deemed it inexpedient to make a present nomination, since the delegates had no authority to do so, and especially since more time was necessary for Antimasonry to spread and for opinion to crystalize on a candidate; (3) As to time, place and manner for the nominations, the report closed with a resolution " That, it is recommended to the people of the United States, opposed to secret societies, to meet in convention on Monday, the 26th day of September, 1831, at the city of Baltimore, by delegates equal in number to their representatives in both houses of Congress, to make nominations . . . for . . . president and vice-president, to be supported at the next election; and for the transaction of such other business as the cause of Anti-masonry may require." [33]

All the various committees having reported, the address to the people of the United States was read and adopted, the convention recommended the utmost vigilance and activity to local committees, appointed a national corresponding committee, and adjourned *sine die*.[34]

This first national convention of a political party's delegates established several important precedents. It adopted from the state convention the chairman pro tempore, the permanent chairman, the several vice-presidents for honorary purposes and the address to the people, the latter the germ of the future platform. It applied on a national scale the appointment of delegates according to the electoral strength of the basic unit, in this case the state, a quota which had been first adopted by the Pennsylvania state convention in 1824 and generally followed by subsequent state conventions. It introduced the roll call of delegates by states, the rules committee, the order-of-business committee, the conduct of its business through the committee system, and most important of all, the resort to the nominating convention for selecting its presidential ticket.

We have seen the reasons why no presidential nomination was attempted by the Philadelphia convention, and that one of these was the need for time in which to fix upon a candidate. The party leaders' preference for Clay had received little encouragement; [35] on the other hand McLean had assured them that he was not a Mason.[36] The latter was encouraging, the more so since McLean was not unpopular throughout the country. Indeed, had the Philadelphia convention made a nomination, McLean would most probably have been its choice,[37] particularly as signs were beginning

[33] Ibid.
[34] Ibid.; The Antimasonic Review, II, vol. x, p. 317.
[35] Weed, Autobiography, pp. 350-352.
[36] McLean to George W. Harris, May 24, 1830, McLean MSS.
[37] B. W. Richards to McLean, September 20, 1830, McLean MSS.; Seward, Autobiography, p. 79.

to appear that the National Republicans intended to head their ticket with Clay.[38]   As it was not certain that McLean would accept the nomination, it is not surprising that he was sounded further, that Richard Rush was approached, that John Quincy Adams was appealed to, while at the same time Clay's course was being hopefully watched during the interval between the Philadelphia and Baltimore conventions.

Clay himself in 1830 believed that Antimasonry would not be a serious obstacle to his success and counted upon the support of the Antimasons; indeed he was even willing to have his party assist their state ticket in New York in return for support from their presidential electors.[39]   He overlooked the fact that it would be difficult for even such politicians as Weed and Tracy to line up their party behind him without some utterance from him against Masonry to aid them in the task.   This he was unwilling to give.[40]   Consequently as time went on and he was nominated by one National Republican meeting after another, and still no Antimasonic statement came from him, the Antimasons turned more and more away from him.[41]   Thus by April, 1831, John Sergeant was writing to Webster that the Antimasons were against Clay only less definitely than they were against Jackson,[42] and by the end of May that year a motion to instruct the Pennsylvania delegates to the Antimasonic convention in Baltimore against Clay was amended to omit his name only after a struggle.[43]   By the end of June, 1831, Clay had definitely given up hope of an Antimasonic endorsement at Baltimore and was trusting that that party, seeing later the futility of success, would withdraw their candidate, in which case he rather than Jackson would receive their support.[44]

[38] Niles' Register, vol. xxxviii, p. 432; cf. Barnes, Memoir of Weed, pp. 39–40.
[39] Clay to John Bailhache, November 24, 1830, Clay, Correspondence, pp. 288–289; Clay to Brooke, June 24, 1830, ibid., pp. 263–264.
[40] Niles' Register, vol. xli, p. 260.
[41] Weed, Autobiography, p. 389.
[42] John Sergeant to Webster, April 9, 1831, Webster MSS.
[43] Niles' Register, vol. xl, p. 237.
[44] Clay to Brooke, June 23, 1831; Clay to Adam Beatty, June 25, 1831, Clay, Correspondence, pp. 303–305.

During the first half of 1831 Richard Rush was considered as a possible nominee by the Antimasons. On April 26, the correspondence committee of York County, Pennsylvania, wrote asking him if he was a Mason and his views upon that subject. He replied satisfactorily and at great length, stating in positive terms that though he had once been a Mason, he had withdrawn from the order before 1826, and was wholly opposed to it as dangerous to republican government and therefore favorable to efforts to put it down.[45] This was of course entirely satisfactory to the Antimasons, but before the end of August he made known to their leaders that he would decline if nominated by the Baltimore convention.[46] Whether this unwillingness was due to Rush's devotion to the National Republicans, to a belief that the Antimasonic ticket could not succeed, or to aversion to further public life, is uncertain.

At the eleventh hour, about two weeks before the Baltimore convention assembled, the Antimasonic leaders in New York, as urged by those in Massachusetts, approached John Quincy Adams to ascertain if he would accept their nomination. For this purpose they sent Tracy and Seward to confer with him. He assented without enthusiasm, expressing a preference to the contrary, adding that he would accept a nomination only upon condition that no other man could command as many of the convention's votes. He also manifested considerable reluctance to detract in any manner from support which might be accorded Clay as National Republican candidate.[47]

While McLean had stated that he had never been connected with the Masonic order, his position in regard to it was not entirely satisfactory inasmuch as he had said that, knowing nothing of its doctrines, he could neither approve

---

[45] These letters are in the Antimasonic Pamphlets of the Maryland Historical Society.

[46] Adams, Memoirs, vol. viii, p. 403.

[47] Adams, ibid., pp. 400–401, 403, 412–413; Seward, Autobiography, pp. 198, 205–206.

nor condemn them.[48] Accordingly Robert Hanna, one of the party leaders in Ohio, wrote with the Baltimore convention in view, asking McLean's sentiments as to Free Masonry.[49] To this the latter replied substantially as he had done to Harris, adding however, " I am in principle opposed to all combinations of men under whatever name or profession, who attempt to control the public will for the attainment of selfish objects."[50] This was more satisfactory to the Antimasons and from this time his stock rose steadily with them, and during the summer of 1831 he gave Weed and Tracy to understand that he was not averse to being nominated at Baltimore.[51] There was a string to this, however. McLean was not minded to resign from the Supreme Bench to become the leader of a forlorn hope, hence he had attached to his acceptance the proviso " In case there should be no other candidate against General Jackson."[52] In his readiness to accept on this condition he was actuated by the hope that the National Republicans, in their eagerness to defeat Jackson, would unite with the Antimasons in supporting him as the opposition candidate. His hopes of this combination were raised when, in the August elections, the Jacksonians secured eight of the twelve congressional seats contested in Clay's own State, and it was suggested that Clay might be kept out of the presidential race in consequence.[53]

The first national nominating convention assembled at Baltimore, Monday, September 26, 1831, in the Athenaeum.[54] Such a convention was enough of a novelty to crowd the city hotels with delegates and spectators.[55] The total number of delegates was 116, accredited from the thirteen States

[48] McLean to Harris, May 24, 1830, McLean MSS.
[49] Robert Hanna to McLean, October 11, 1830, McLean MSS.
[50] McLean to Hanna, ——, 1830, McLean MSS.
[51] Weed to McLean, August 23, 1831, McLean MSS.
[52] Weed, Autobiography, p. 389.
[53] Niles' Register, vol. xli, p. 1; Weed to McLean, August 23, 1831; M. T. Simpson to McLean, August 26, 1831, McLean MSS.
[54] The Athenaeum was on the southwest corner of St. Paul and Lexington Streets (J. T. Scharf, Chronicles of Baltimore, p. 408).
[55] Baltimore Gazette, September 26, 27, 1831.

of Maine, New Hampshire, Vermont, Massachusetts, Rhode Island, Connecticut, New York, New Jersey, Pennsylvania, Delaware, Maryland, Ohio and Indiana. Only the New York, Massachusetts and Pennsylvania delegations were equal in numbers to the prescribed ratio; hence, like that at Philadelphia, this convention was entirely controlled by these three states. Indeed, judging by its proceedings and the personnel of its committees, the New York leaders, seconded by those of Massachusetts, played the directing rôle.[56] Except Ohio with nine, no other State had more than six delegates present, and Maryland, Delaware, New Hampshire and Indiana had but one each.

The Baltimore convention, except for the nominations, introduced little in the way of organization and procedure that had not been put into practice at Philadelphia. This statement applies to the temporary and the permanent chairman, the several vice-presidents and secretaries, and the committee organization to conduct the business of the meeting. The one innovation, aside from the nominations, was the examination of the delegates' credentials, which was not done by a committee, but by the officers in full convention. This in itself was not a new idea, but, like the nominating proceedings, was adopted from past state convention practice. One other noteworthy feature was the assignment of special places in the hall to the " reporters of the convention's proceedings." [57]

On Monday afternoon business began in earnest with the report of Phelps of Massachusetts, chairman of the committee on business, which comprised one member from each State and was entrusted with bringing before the convention necessary business. After citing the call by the Philadelphia convention of the present meeting, he recommended the appointment of six separate committees, whose respective functions were: to report on Masonic penalties, to compile a

[56] Proceedings of the Baltimore Antimasonic Convention, in Antimasonic Pamphlets, Maryland Historical Society.
[57] Proceedings of the Baltimore Antimasonic Convention.

list of Masonic obstructions of the proceedings against Morgan's murderers, to express the convention's views on Masonry, to raise funds, to publish the proceedings of this and of the Philadelphia convention, and to prepare an address to the people of the United States.

Phelps' committee made two other recommendations, one calling for a report from the party's national corresponding committee,[58] the other containing the rules for governing the nominating proceedings. The latter provided that next day at noon, Tuesday, the nominations for president and vice-president should be made and "that the votes be taken by ballot separately for each of those candidates, and that the votes of three-fourths of all the members present, be considered necessary to constitute a choice."[59]   Each of the above recommendations was considered in turn and was adopted. Thus originated the practice of requiring more than a simple majority to indicate the party's choice of a candidate. This precedent, modified to a two-thirds majority, was followed by the Democratic convention eight months later, and by every subsequent convention of that party thereafter. Who it was that originated it in the Antimasonic order-of-business committee is unknown.[60]

The Antimasonic delegates came to Baltimore with the nomination of McLean a foregone conclusion among their leaders. All that was necessary to secure for him a unanimous choice as the party's candidate was his final announcement that he would accept.[61] Weed and Tracy had been led to believe that he would certainly accept[62] and Thaddeus Stevens, who had also been in communication with him, was positive of it.[63] Indeed the rumor afloat in Baltimore during the Sunday immediately before the convention was

[58] Composed of Henry Dana Ward and two others, all of New York City.
[59] Proceedings of the Baltimore Antimasonic Convention.
[60] Ibid.
[61] Richards to McLean, October 1, 1831, McLean MSS.
[62] Weed, to McLean, August 23, 1831, McLean MSS.
[63] Seward, Autobiography, p. 89.

that McLean would be its choice for president, with William Wirt for vice-president, the only uncertainty being as to the latter's accepting.[64]

Late that Sunday evening came the letter in which McLean promised to make known his final decision as to the nomination.[65] It was a politely firm refusal. The reasons alleged were that as Jackson, Clay and Calhoun were already before the people, the addition of a fourth candidate would merely "distract still more the public mind," and therefore "be injurious to . . . the country" by entailing the choice by the House of Representatives of another minority president. He added further that as a member of the Supreme Court, he ought not to enter upon such a political enterprise "unless the use of his name would be likely to tranquilize the public mind."[66] Thus his ground for refusal was plainly his belief that he had no chance of success, because of Clay's entry into the field as National Republican candidate, a fact which he had recently ascertained.[67]

McLean's refusal was a heavy and disconcerting blow to the Antimasons. No one knew what the result would be and a hundred rumors were speedily afloat. One of these was that John Quincy Adams would be nominated; another stated that Wirt would be the nominee.[68] Seward says that the refusal "fell like a wet blanket upon our warm expectations." The convention "felt that it could derive no strength or prestige from a nomination of one of its own well-known and practiced leaders. It needed a new name, not before identified with its history, and a high name at that."[69]

Nothing daunted, the resourceful party leaders, according to Seward, set themselves to work, "inasmuch as we could

[64] Letter to the Washington Journal from a correspondent, in Baltimore Gazette, September 27, 1831.

[65] Weed, Autobiography, pp. 389–390.

[66] McLean's letter in Niles' Register, vol. xli, pp. 259–260; Weed, Autobiography, pp. 389–390.

[67] Weed, Autobiography, p. 389; Seward, Autobiography, p. 89.

[68] Letter to Washington Journal in Baltimore Gazette, September 27, 1831.

[69] Seward, Autobiography, p. 90.

not find a candidate, to make one." [70]   Weed, Tracy and
Spencer, all from New York, and Phelps from Massachusetts, immediately sounded both John Marshall and William
Wirt.[71]   The indications are that they preferred Marshall,
for a resolution passed the convention Monday evening inviting him to attend its deliberations, while the proceedings
record no such action in Wirt's case.[72]   Marshall accepted
the invitation to be present as a spectator, but evidently
would not hear to having his name presented for nomination.   Wirt, however, as well as Barbour, Forsyth and Archer of the Jackson party, among others visited the convention Tuesday, the second day.[73]   It was this diligent search
for a candidate which led the convention to postpone making
the nominations from Tuesday until Wednesday.[74]

The labors of the party leaders were more successful with
Wirt than with Marshall. Tuesday evening a confidential
letter was received from the former stating his readiness to
accept the nomination " upon the terms we had avowed." [75]
What conditions had been named to Wirt as necessary to his
nomination, is uncertain, but judging from the tenor of his
public letter of acceptance, they must have been very general with little or no stress laid upon an Antimasonic program.

Seward's account of Wirt's nomination is corroborated by
Weed [76] and is doubtless correct. Seward says:

Wirt had been a Mason, and a large party in the convention
were unwilling to assign him the place of standard-bearer upon a
conversion which they thought sudden and interested. Others
were of the opinion that, notwithstanding Judge McLean's declining, we might safely force the nomination upon him. It was in the
maintenance of these opinions that I found Thaddeus Stevens . . .
unreasonable and impracticable. It was assigned to me to combat
them in private caucus. We debated the subject until midnight

[70] Ibid.
[71] Ibid.:Weed, Autobiography, pp. 390–391.
[72] Proceedings of the Baltimore Antimasonic Convention.
[73] Baltimore Gazette, September 28, 1831.
[74] Proceedings of the Baltimore Antimasonic Convention.
[75] Seward, Autobiography, p. 90.
[76] Weed, Autobiography, p. 391.

and adjourned under an apprehension that the convention would explode next day. . . . I lodged that night in a room with Mr. Stevens. When I awoke in the morning, filled with anxiety which last night's debates had left, I was surprised to find that my fellow lodger was entirely calm and undisturbed. I remonstrated with him against his pertinacious adhesion to Mr. McLean, and so far prevailed with him as to obtain an assurance of his acquiescence in the nomination of Mr. Wirt, if that should be the choice of the convention.[77]

Thanks to the efforts of Weed, Tracy, Spencer and Phelps with Wirt, and to those of Seward with Stevens, all was harmony when the convention took up the nominations on Wednesday. There were no nominating speeches. Phelps and Stevens were appointed tellers to receive and count the ballots. On the vote for presidential nominee, each delegate rose as his name was called and deposited his ballot in an open box on the tellers' table in the center of the hall. When all had voted the number of ballots was checked against the number of delegates present and found to correspond. Phelps then opened each ballot, read it aloud and passed it to Stevens who checked it, the secretaries keeping count meanwhile. The results, announced by the president of the convention,[78] showed Wirt to have 108 of the 111 votes cast, 27 more than the necessary three-fourths. On Stevens' motion, Wirt was by acclamation declared unanimously nominated—much as is done in present-day conventions. Similar action, by ballot followed by acclamation, resulted in the nomination of Amos Ellmaker for vice-president. The latter, though not mentioned in the convention's earlier proceedings, had been prominent in the Philadelphia Convention, and had probably been selected outside of the convention. Two committees of three each were then appointed to notify Wirt and Ellmaker of their respective nominations.[79]

---

[77] Seward, Autobiography, pp. 90–91.

[78] John C. Spencer, a prominent lawyer of New York State, a recent convert to the cause of Antimasonry, was president of the convention.

[79] Proceedings of the Baltimore Antimasonic Convention.

Wirt's letter of acceptance arrived that evening at eight o'clock. It was at once read before the convention, ordered entered on the minutes, and the meeting voted that he be recommended to the country for cordial support as the Antimasonic candidate. For all this, Wirt's letter must have been hard to stomach. He accepted the nomination as a personal honor from a distinguished body, tendered him for personal considerations purely, and not upon Antimasonic principles involving a crusade against Masonry. He stated that he had once been a Mason, but had never advanced far in the order, and had gradually lost interest and dropped out, though from no conviction against it; that he did not believe the Masonic complicity in the Morgan case to be a characteristic or generally authorized proceeding of the order, and ended by saying that if, knowing these sentiments, the convention desired to change its nomination, he should retire with even more pleasure than he accepted. From all of which it appears that so far from being eager for the nomination, Wirt was entirely indifferent to it save as an honor accorded his personal character and attainments, and that if elected he proposed to enter upon no proscriptive program against Masonry as an institution.[80]

Only one other interesting action was taken. It was the adoption of a resolution providing for another convention of the party to be held in Washington in September, 1835, to consider such subjects as the cause of Antimasonry might require—no specific mention made of nominations—"unless the National Antimasonic Committee shall otherwise advise."[81] Here is the beginning of the present-day practice of entrusting to the party's national committee the power of issuing the call and settling the time and place for its national convention. As has been noted, it was applied on a state scale by the Antimasons in New York in 1828. The

---

[80] Ibid.; Niles' Register, vol. xli, pp. 83–85.
[81] Niles' Register, ibid., p. 85; Baltimore Gazette, September 29, 1831.

Baltimore convention merely followed the state precedent by adopting it on a national scale.

These and other proceedings such as the reappointment of the national corresponding committee, with the same personnel and powers as before, the reading and adoption of the platform—the address to the people, as it was called—were not completed until midnight.[82] The convention had previously fixed this day, Wednesday, the 28th, for adjournment, hence this first of night sessions in national convention practice.[83]

This first application of the nominating convention to national party politics established permanently this means of selecting presidential candidates. No particular credit for an innovation accrues to the Antimasons, for the idea had been in the country's political atmosphere for eight years past. The organization of the convention, its business procedure, the ratio of delegate representation, the address to the people, were all adopted directly from, or else enlarged applications of, like practices in the state nominating conventions, dating from that in Pennsylvania which nominated Jackson in 1824. In some details this Antimasonic convention and that at Philadelphia in 1830 seem to have been the pioneers. Among their innovations may be named the rules committee, the greater stress on delegates' credentials, the order-of-business committee, the conduct of business by means of the committee system, and the unanimous confirmation of the candidate by acclamation after the ballot.

This convention was a true nominating body, but became so more by an unforeseen contingency than by design. It assembled with the choice of McLean practically predetermined, and it was only when his eleventh hour refusal threw upon the convention the immediate and urgent necessity of making a de facto selection that the meeting became, perforce, a nominating convention in the present-day sense of the word.

[82] Seward, Autobiography, p. 208.
[83] Proceedings of the Baltimore Antimasonic Convention.

CHAPTER III

THE NATIONAL REPUBLICANS

Jackson's sweeping victory in November, 1828, left the National Republicans temporarily at a standstill concerning their future course as a party. Like political parties today they preferred to attribute their defeat to their leader's personality rather than to any dislike by the nation as a whole for nationalism and the "American System." Adams' defeat automatically removed him from the leadership, and with one accord the eyes of the party turned to Henry Clay as "the Nation's only hope."[1]

For the time being after the election, Clay himself had nothing definite to recommend beyond a watchful waiting for the new administration to make mistakes, or for a schism to develop among its followers. Of this last he was quite confident. His letter to Webster of November 30, 1828, reveals the situation as follows:

We are of the majority in regard to measures; we are of the minority in respect to the person designated as C. Magistrate. . . . I think in regard to the new Administration, we should alike avoid professions of support or declarations of opposition, in advance. We can only yield the former, if our principles are adopted and pursued. . . . On the other hand, if we were now to issue a manifesto of hostility, we should keep united, by a sense of common danger, the discordant Confederates, who have taken the field against us. They cannot remain in Corps but from external pressure. The dissensions among them this winter, the formation of the new Cabinet, and the Inaugural Speech will enable us to discover the whole ground of future operations. . . . I shall retire to Ashland after the 4th of March and there consider . . . my future course.[2]

Such was the program for the immediate future and it was followed until near the end of the congressional session

---

[1] The Marylander [Baltimore], November 19, 1828.
[2] Clay to Webster, November 30, 1828, Webster MSS.

of 1829–1830. Clay's letter reveals incidentally a decided underestimation of Jackson's inherent ability as a leader, and a still greater failure to comprehend the latter's strength in Clay's own West, the chief cause of Adams' downfall in 1828. According to his plan, Clay retired to private life in March, 1829, where he remained nominally until his election to the Senate in November, 1831. For all his retirement during this time, he was careful to keep in the public eye, for he spoke frequently at public meetings, dinners and barbecues.[3] In January, 1830, he made a trip to New Orleans, ostensibly to visit a married daughter,[4] spent about two months there and returned up the river in March, being accorded many enthusiastic attentions.[5]

While Clay was thus keeping in public notice, Webster in the Senate was watching sharply the administration's course with an eye to a suitable campaign issue, or any favorable grounds for attack. Jackson's removals from, and appointments to, office, and the Eaton affair, while suitable for campaign ammunition as proof of the administration's incompetence, were obviously not of sufficient national or constitutional importance to serve as leading campaign issues.[6] The struggle between the Calhoun and Van Buren groups of the Jacksonians, and the impending break between the President and Calhoun, Webster regarded hopefully as portending a division in the Democratic ranks " that might lead to some beneficial results," [7] particularly should Jackson not again be a candidate. As the President's course was then, April 6, 1830, uncertain, National Republican tactics for the future were compelled in some degree to await further developments.

---

[3] Clay to Josiah S. Johnston, October 8, 1829, Clay, Correspondence, p. 245.

[4] Niles' Register, vol xxxvii, p. 399.

[5] Ibid., vol. xxxvii, p. 429; vol. xxxviii, pp. 4, 48, 105.

[6] Webster, Correspondence, vol. i, p. 483.

[7] Clay to J. S. Johnston, April 6, 1830, Clay, Correspondence, p. 253.

On April 18, five days after the Jefferson anniversary dinner had revealed Jackson and Calhoun at opposites as to nullification, Webster wrote Clay his opinion that the President intended to stand for reelection.[8] Some days after this letter, Clay wrote to Judge Brooke, his manager in Virginia, giving the following estimate of the future:

If Jackson loses either New York, Pennsylvania, or Virginia, he will be defeated. If he unites the votes of all three . . . he will succeed. And I have generally supposed that the degrees of probability of loss to him of those States were in the order in which I have placed them. If I am right he is most certain of Virginia. . . . In New York some progress has been made toward effecting a union of the various parties opposed to the present administration but the problem is yet to be solved whether such an union can be accomplished. . . . The whole case presents one encouraging view. Jackson has lost, is losing, and must continue to lose.[9]

Toward the end of the 1829–1830 session of Congress the National Republicans made the first definite campaign move. The party's policy centered in the " American System," comprising protectionist tariff and internal improvements—the latter chiefly in the form of roads and canals—at national expense. The high tariff of 1828 had raised a storm of indignation in the South, but as the administration showed no signs of revising it downward, the National Republicans turned to internal improvements, a subject in which Pennsylvania and the whole West were supposed to be greatly interested.

Internal improvements at national expense, aside from the particularistic South, were not unpopular in the country at large. Indeed a general system of such improvement had been gaining steadily in popularity since Monroe's time. In Pennsylvania, the keystone of Jackson's political strength, the large Quaker element was already irritated at the administration's Indian removal policy. Moreover there was in the State a large group of local politicians and contractors

---

[8] Webster to Clay, April 18, 1830, Clay, Correspondence, pp. 259–260.

[9] Clay to Francis Brooke, April 24, 1830, Clay, Correspondence, pp. 263–264.

whose considerable influence was exerted on public opinion in favor of roads and canals. Such improvements would also be welcome in the West.[10] Jackson's attitude was not definitely known on the subject, as it had not been previously made clear, but owing to the Pennsylvania situation and the supposed attitude of the West, it was not believed that he would dare to act openly and decidedly against projects of internal improvements, even if he disapproved of the principle which sought to finance them from the federal treasury.[11]

The National Republicans needed an issue upon which to launch their campaign, and as the tariff was not immediately available they turned to the second part of the "American System," internal improvements. Thus the party in Congress gave its attention to several such bills then pending, of which the Maysville Road bill was destined to become the most prominent. Jackson's first annual message had shown a tendency toward strict construction of the federal power relating to such measures.[12] The probabilities appear to be that the National Republicans hoped to obtain from his attitude toward internal improvements a leading issue upon which to launch and conduct the coming presidential campaign.[13]

A letter from Webster to Clay at the time the Maysville Road bill was in Jackson's hands, but before its return with his veto, throws further light upon the situation:

> On the whole, my dear sir, I think a crisis is arriving, or rather has arrived. . . . Parties, must now, necessarily, be started out anew; and the great ground of difference will be the Tariff and Internal Improvements. You are necessarily at the head of one party, and General Jackson will be, if he is not already, identified with the other. The question will be put to the country. Let the country decide it.[14]

---

10 Van Buren, Autobiography, pp. 305, 309.
11 Ibid., pp. 313–315, 320, 325.
12 Richardson, Messages and Papers, vol. ii, pp. 451–453.
13 Webster to Clay, May 23, 1830, Clay, Correspondence, pp. 275–276.
14 Ibid.

A fortnight earlier, while the Maysville bill was still in the House of Representatives, Clay had written to his friend, Josiah S. Johnston, Senator from Louisiana, expressing hopes that the Senate would pass it, and that New England Senators especially would support it. "We shall then," he wrote, "be able practically to know who are our real friends."[15]

The letter of Webster just mentioned also throws light upon the plan for opening the campaign. "I think," he wrote Clay, "you cannot be kept back from the contest. The people will bring you out, nolens volens. Let them do it." After advising Clay to abstain, for political effect, from visiting the North at this time, the writer continued, "You will hear from the North, every town and village in it, on the 4th of July."

On May 27, 1830, Jackson returned the Maysville bill to the House of Representatives with his veto,[16] noting the following objections: (1) The construction of internal improvements by federal authority was unconstitutional; (2) Appropriations of money by the national government to aid works of internal improvement must be limited solely to works of a national, as opposed to a local, or state character, in order to be constitutional; (3) The present bill, it pointed out, appropriated money to aid a road purely local in character; (4) It was inexpedient to make any extensive appropriations, even for similar works which were national in character until the public debt should be paid and the Constitution amended to define the national power to that effect.[17]

Jackson and Van Buren had been watching closely the internal improvement sentiment both in and outside of Congress. By the end of April, 1830, Jackson was definitely resolved upon administering a decisive check to this sentiment and to this end had instructed Van Buren to watch such internal improvement bills as were pending in Congress

[15] Clay to Johnston, May 9, 1830, ibid., p. 267.
[16] Niles' Register, vol. xxxviii, p. 271.
[17] Richardson, Messages and Papers, vol. ii, pp. 483–493.

in order to select the one whose veto would affect the smallest number of voters.[18] The bill authorizing an appropriation for the purchase of stock in the "Maysville . . . Turnpike Road Company" was the one Van Buren selected. The road in question was wholly within Kentucky, and therefore local in character, and had the added incentive of being in Clay's State. Indeed Jackson, who had doubtless been observing the enemy closely, was of the opinion that Clay and his party were pushing forward this particular measure primarily for political effect, and hence was the more ready to accept such a challenge.[19]

The National Republicans immediately seized upon this as a campaign issue. The veto was attacked savagely in the House by Stanberry, Vance and Kennon, all from Ohio, and was warmly defended by Barbour of Virginia and by Polk and Bell of Tennessee.[20] The attacks were mainly of a denunciatory character, paying but little attention to the constitutional objections urged in the veto. Characteristic of these denunciations was Stanberry's statement that the veto represented the views of the President's ministry rather than those of the executive himself, because the hand of the "great magician" was visible in every line of the message.[21]

The Maysville veto coming on the heels of the rising discontent among Calhoun's friends, was promptly utilized by the National Republicans for campaign purposes, as they hoped to annex such elements of the Jacksonians as would not follow the President's lead on the subject of internal improvements. Indeed, there was ground for hope, as the vote in the House of Representatives had been 97 to 90 in favor of passing the bill over the President's veto,[22] and

---

[18] Van Buren, Autobiography, p. 320.
[19] Ibid., pp. 320–325; cf. Niles' Register, vol. xxxviii, p. 218.
[20] Niles' Register, vol. xxxviii, pp. 281, 309–315.
[21] Ibid., p. 309; Van Buren, Autobiography, p. 329.
[22] Clay to Webster, June 7, 1830, Webster, Correspondence, vol. i, pp. 504–505; Niles' Register, vol. xxxviii, p. 281.

many of Jackson's party managers feared its effects upon his popularity and their party.[23]

As soon as the veto was known the National Republican press began thundering against it.[24] According to Clay's plan [25] his friends in Kentucky took advantage of the feeling aroused in the State by the veto,[26] and held a large public meeting at Lexington on June 21, at which the President's course was roundly denounced, and a constitutional amendment recommended to curb the executive veto by enabling a majority vote to over-ride it.[27] On July 4, according to schedule,[28] the campaign designed to elect Clay president was simultaneously launched in the North and West, while at Washington a large meeting of Clay's friends was held for the same purpose.[29] In all the meetings, banquets and toasts devoted to this end, endorsement of Clay and internal improvements and denunciation of the veto figured prominently.[30] Referring to National Republican tactics at this time, Ingham wrote to Jackson—who was then at the Hermitage—from Washington, "The opposition are certainly preparing for a more violent contest than even the last. Their pens are dipped in Gall, and no effort will be left untried to carry the war as Mr. Clay says into ' every hamlet.' "[31]

Following up this beginning, Clay, during the latter part of July, addressed a public meeting at Columbus, Ohio, and again, on August 3, delivered a long speech at Cincinnati. In this latter, after carefully side-stepping a request for his views as to rechartering the United States Bank, he extolled

[23] Van Buren, Autobiography, pp. 324–325.
[24] Niles' Register, vol. xxxviii, p. 269.
[25] Clay to Webster, June 7, 1830, Webster, Correspondence, vol. i, pp. 504–505.
[26] Niles' Register, vol. xxxviii, p. 366.
[27] Ibid., pp. 337, 406–412.
[28] Webster to Clay, May 23, 1830, Clay, Correspondence, pp. 275–276.
[29] Niles, Register, vol. xxxviii, p. 365.
[30] Ibid.
[31] Ingham to Jackson, July 25, 1830, Jackson MSS.

the " American System," especially its internal improvement
side, and then assailed the Maysville veto, chiefly on the
ground that it was inconsistent with Jackson's previous votes
in Congress and had proceeded from an irresponsible cabinet's control of the President.[32] He followed these speeches
with a short tour through Ohio, Indiana and Kentucky,
partly, no doubt, for effect upon the approaching fall elections.[33]

On the same day as his Cincinnati speech, in Delaware [34]
Clay was nominated for president by " a convention of the
national republicans of this state." This was followed in
September by a like action in Connecticut,[35] and on December 9, 1830, he was nominated by a large convention in his
own State.[36] With the campaign thus launched, it remained
to keep it moving, to keep up interest, and to organize the
party for more general efforts.

On December 13, the National Republicans of New York
City held a meeting some 2,500 strong, and, after endorsing
the various nominations of Clay, provided for the holding of
local ward meetings of the party all over the city. These
local meetings were to establish ward committees as a means
of stirring up party interest, and were to designate five members each as a part of a general committee " to superintend
the concerns of the national republican party of this city." [37]
The general committee thus established was about seventy
strong. With William H. Ireland as chairman, it soon un-
dertook in addition to its local objects the effective organization of the party throughout the State.[38]

It was general knowledge that the Antimasons had plans
laid for their nominating convention in Baltimore in Sep-

---

[32] Niles' Register, vol. xxxviii, p. 417; vol. xxxix, pp. 25–32.
[33] Ibid., vol. xxxviii, p. 477.
[34] Ibid., vol. xxxviii, p. 432.
[35] Ibid., vol. xxxix, p. 94.
[36] Ibid., pp. 90, 302.
[37] New York American, December 14, 1830, in Niles' Register,
vol. xxxix, p. 303.
[38] National Intelligencer, January 4, February 17, 1831.

tember, 1831. This means for choosing a candidate seems to have been spontaneously adopted by the National Republicans in several States during February, 1831. There was this difference, however,—the Antimasons in projecting their nominating convention actually did intend it as a means of choosing a candidate from among several possibilities, while the National Republicans were not seriously considering any candidate but Clay. Hence the party's move for a nominating convention was purely for propagandic purposes, to stir up further enthusiasm for Clay whose nomination, by any convention that might be planned, was a foregone conclusion from the outset.

The first move for such a convention came from the abovementioned general committee of New York City. In the process of working out an effective party organization in the State, it recommended on February 9, 1831, that a state convention be held at Albany in June to endorse and support Clay "and that the National Convention be held at Philadelphia the first Wednesday in September next." [39] The obvious purpose for the choice of this particular time was to forestall and influence the Antimasons who had considered Clay, and whose nominating convention was scheduled for Baltimore on the third Monday in September.

The party's central organ, the National Intelligencer, found the convention suggestion good, but advised that it be held later in the year so as to be able to act according to the latest political developments, and also recommended that it should be held nearer to Washington, at Baltimore for example, for the convenience of the members of Congress who might be delegates. The Intelligencer professed its entire willingness that these points be determined by the party state conventions.[40] These two points were speedily settled almost simultaneously by Maryland, Connecticut and Maine. In Maryland a legislative caucus of National Republicans met

[39] Ibid., February 17, 1831.
[40] Ibid.

February 17, and recommended that each congressional district in the state elect a delegate " to meet in general convention at Baltimore, on the second Monday in December next." The meeting then appointed two delegates at large and further extended invitation to " our brethren of other states who . . . deprecate the reelection of Andrew Jackson," to do likewise " by delegates equal in number to the electors of president to which their states are entitled in order to present as candidates for the presidency and vice-presidency, statesmen the best established in public confidence." [41] The National Intelligencer found this quite satisfactory and stated that it met with the approval of the party leaders in Washington.[42]

Before this news had time to reach New England a state convention in Connecticut also recommended that the convention " be held in Baltimore in December next," without naming the day, but prescribed the States' respective electoral strength as the basis for regulating the size of delegations ; [43] similar action was taken by a legislative caucus in Maine.[44] The matter was finally settled by the endorsement of the Maryland proposal by a great National Republican meeting, 800 strong, which met in Philadelphia, April 4, with John Sergeant presiding.[45]

All this activity was the more necessary since the fall elections in 1830 had made little change in the party situation, neither Clay nor Jackson being either greatly weakened or greatly strengthened thereby. The fears and doubts of some of Jackson's subordinates as to the effect of the Maysville veto on the country, had not been realized. The main hope of the National Republicans for favorable results from the veto had been based on its expected effects in New York, Pennsylvania and the West. In this they were considerably

---

[41] Annapolis Republican, February 19, 1831, in Niles' Register, vol. xl, pp. 28-29.
[42] National Intelligencer, February 24, 1831.
[43] Ibid., March 7, 1831.
[44] Ibid.
[45] Niles' Register, vol. xl, pp. 127-128.

disappointed. New York and Pennsylvania were building their own roads and canals and this fact went far to neutralize the effect of the veto; indeed, Jackson had been perceptibly strengthened by it in New York.[46] In the West, generally speaking, the effects of the veto on Ohio and Kentucky were favorable to the National Republicans, but did not give either state wholly to them.[47] Outside these two States the veto's effects on the West were beneficial to Jackson rather than otherwise. On his summer trip to the Hermitage, he wrote as the result of his observations, that it worked well, and "has become what my enemies neither wished nor expected, very popular. I have no doubt but it will be sustained by a large majority of the people." [48]

Jackson's intuitive ability to sense the feeling of the masses toward his leading measures was the secret of his strength as party leader and was the despair of the opposition. The President's standing in the country at large was summed up by Felix Grundy, apparently after making a tour of the country. Speaking with direct reference to the veto, he said:

I find that in New Hampshire and Maine the strength of the administration is increased by it . . . has done no harm in Pennsylvania . . . has given strength in New York . . . results in Ohio & Kentucky indeterminate. . . . The result of the matter in my mind is, that altho your friends may not be numerically increased, their attachment is now of a stronger texture—formerly it consisted in a degree in an affection for the man and an admiration of his character & public services and confidence in his virtues—Now is added an adherence to political and republican principles; the former are very good recommendations to get a man into office, and the latter the safest chance for him when in.[49]

In February, 1831, the publication of the break between Jackson and Calhoun, and the disruption of the cabinet which followed in April, improved temporarily the prospects of the National Republicans, particularly in Pennsylvania,[50] and this

---

[46] J. A. Hamilton to Jackson, June 27, 1830, Jackson MSS.; Van Buren to Jackson, July 25, 1830, Van Buren MSS.

[47] Moses Dawson to Jackson, July 5, 1830, Grundy to Jackson, July 31, 1830, Jackson MSS.

[48] Jackson to Van Buren, June 26, July 12, 1830, Van Buren MSS.

[49] Grundy to Jackson, July 31, 1830, Jackson MSS.

[50] Richards to McLean, June 24, 1831, McLean MSS.

naturally aroused their hopes of adding to their party the disgruntled Calhoun partizans in addition to the fragments shorn from the Democrats by the Maysville veto. Although Van Buren's resignation from the cabinet mystified them [51] and deprived them temporarily of one of their favorite objects of attack, this did not prevent them from making every effort to exploit the unprecedented cabinet change to their advantage and to make the most of the fierce newspaper recriminations during the ensuing summer between the administration supporters and the ejected secretaries.[52]

Between April and November, 1831, eighteen States and the District of Columbia elected delegates to the convention in December.[53]   The specified quota per State was, as it had been with the Antimasons, and as the party legislative caucuses had recommended, equal to its electoral college strength. As far as can be ascertained the delegates were chosen on this basis either by state convention, as in New York and Ohio,[54] by state legislative caucus, as in Massachusetts and New Hampshire,[55] or by leaving the choice entirely to the individual congressional district with the two delegates at large appointed by caucus, as in Virginia, Maryland, Pennsylvania and Maine.[56] Of the eighteen States that chose delegates only Massachusetts, Rhode Island, New Jersey, Delaware, Maryland, Virginia and Kentucky were represented by their full quota of delegates. Of the other States, New York, Pennsylvania and Ohio were represented by 17, 23 and 18 delegates respectively. Of four others, North Carolina, Tennessee, Louisiana and Indiana, none had more than three delegates present. Apparently it was not thought worth while to instruct any of the delegations, since the only name in the party's collective mind was that of Clay, hence, as noted before, his nomination was a foregone conclusion

[51] Niles' Register, vol. xl, pp. 129, 165.
[52] Ibid., pp. 318, 372–389, passim.
[53] Ibid., vol. xli, pp. 306–307.
[54] Ibid., vol. xl, pp. 254, 279, 401.
[55] Ibid., pp. 293, 353.
[56] Ibid., pp. 28–29, 113, 127, 128; vol. xli, p. 259.

and this convention was mainly for the purpose of stimulating enthusiasm for the party and its candidate.

There was need of such stimulation. The reorganization of Jackson's cabinet in the summer of 1831 had eliminated the Eaton scandal as a ground of attack, and the group of able and intelligent gentlemen whom Jackson summoned to the new cabinet had decidedly strengthened the administration in the country at large.[57] Furthermore the Maysville veto had not reacted nearly as much to Jackson's disadvantage as the National Republicans had anticipated. A letter from William Carroll, governor of Tennessee, to Nicholas Biddle at this time, referring to Jackson's strength in the West stated, " his popularity remains much as it was in most of the Western country." [58] Moreover, Clay had refused from motives of " principle and policy " to make any statement or declaration which would conciliate the Antimasons,[59] and in September they entered the field as a national party behind Wirt, thus dividing the potential opposition to Jackson. Another ground for pessimism was the fact that in spite of the efforts of the managers in New York, the National Republican party was so weak that the fall elections of 1831 were almost wholly a Democratic-Antimasonic contest.[60] In addition to all this Clay had allowed his state legislature to elect him to the Senate in November,[61] a move the wisdom of which, with the campaign so far advanced, was doubtful. It looked as if he thought that a bird in the hand was worth two in the bush. On the whole the prospect for a successful campaign in 1832 was not at all good.

Clay himself was well aware of this unpromising outlook. He wrote his Virginia manager, Judge Brooke, on December 9, 1831, " The impression is that the Baltimore convention

[57] James Buchanan, Works (J. B. Moore, Ed.), vol. ii, pp. 177–178.
[58] Carroll to Biddle, June 29, 1831, Biddle MSS.
[59] Clay to Brooke, July 18, 1831, Clay, Correspondence, p. 306.
[60] Niles' Register, vol. xli, p. 237.
[61] Ibid.

will make a nomination of me. I wish I could add that the impression was more favorable than it is of the success of such a nomination. Something, however, may turn up (and that must be our encouraging hope) to give a brighter aspect to our affairs." [62] Within a month after the date of this letter, something which will be noticed in a subsequent chapter, did " turn up "—the Bank of the United States.

The National Republican delegates to Baltimore convened at the Athenaeum on Monday, December 12, 1831, with only 135 present,[63] owing to the state of weather and roads. For this reason the principal action on this day was to elect Abner Lacock of Pennsylvania, a former Crawford man who was opposed to Jackson, chairman pro tempore and to adopt a resolution inviting all newspaper editors and reporters to seats set apart for them. The meeting then adjourned till the next day.[64]

Another resolution had provided for the examination of the delegates' credentials by each delegation for itself, and, having done so, each was then to report a list of its personnel to the secretary of the convention on Tuesday. The Tuesday session, therefore, began with a roll call by States which showed 156 members present from seventeen States. John Holmes, delegate and Senator from Maine, then moved that a committee of five be appointed to recommend permanent officers and to " report what further proceedings they might deem necessary." This marks the introduction into our convention practice of the Committee on Permanent Organ-

[62] Clay to Brooke, December 9, 1830, Clay, Correspondence, p. 321.
[63] The total number of delegates attending the convention was 168, from Maine, New Hampshire, Vermont, Massachusetts, Rhode Island, Connecticut, New York, New Jersey, Pennsylvania, Delaware, Maryland, Virginia, Tennessee, North Carolina, Kentucky, Ohio, Indiana, Louisiana and the District of Columbia; cf. Journal of the National Republican Convention, in History Pamphlets, vol. 293, Johns Hopkins University Library.
[64] Niles' Register, vol. xli, p. 301. Niles' Register contains a full account of the convention's proceedings. Hezekiah Niles was present in person during the convention's deliberations. See also Journal of the National Republican Convention.

ization, wherein this convention was followed by the Democrats five months later. The duty to suggest other matters for the convention's consideration was a charge like that of the Antimasonic committee on subjects and order of business. On this, the most important committee in the National Republican convention, were appointed none but party leaders; namely, Holmes of Maine, John Sergeant of Pennsylvania, Henry A. S. Dearborn of Massachusetts, James Thomas of Maryland, and James W. Denny of Kentucky. After a brief interval this committee recommended for permanent president James Barbour of Virginia, a former colleague of Clay in Adams' cabinet, four vice-presidents and two secretaries.[65]

Barbour was then installed and delivered a short speech more nearly " keynote " in character than that in either of the other party conventions.[66] After invitations had been extended to Charles Carroll and other distinguished Baltimoreans to sit within the bar of the convention, Holmes of the organization and order-of-business committee recommended that the convention " do *now* proceed to nominate a candidate for . . . president to be supported by those who are opposed to the reelection of Andrew Jackson." This was adopted and here Barbour laid before the house a letter he had received a day or two earlier from Clay, with the latter's request that it be laid before the convention should his name be brought up as candidate. It was an earnest plea from Clay to the convention to dismiss all thoughts of himself and to weigh with him every man available for nomination solely on the basis of fitness for such a position. Clay's motive in this move is not clear; it may have been a sincere desire to stand in the way of no one who might be deemed more capable of combining back of one man all the elements opposed to Jackson, possibly John McLean; or it may have been designed to dispel the general impression that

---

[65] Niles' Register, vol. xli, p. 301.

[66] Cf. Niles' Register, vol. xli, p. 302, with Antimasonic Convention Proceedings and The Globe of May 23, 1832.

the convention had assembled merely to stimulate interest in his campaign and to nominate him.[67]   Of these two motives the latter seems to me the more probable.

Peter R. Livingston, a recent convert from the New York Democrats, now rose and made the first nominating speech in national convention history. Unfortunately, it is not reported; the fullest record merely says " Mr. Livingston . . . rose, and, after some pertinent and eloquent remarks, nominated *Henry Clay*, which was received with loud and reiterated applause." [68]   On Dearborn's suggestion that convention then adopted what was destined to be the forerunner of the modern practice of voting. The method of choosing nominees in both of the other two conventions had been by secret ballot; here it was by roll call, each delegate rising as called and orally naming the man of his choice. It differed from the present-day method, however, in being a roll call of individual delegates, instead of state delegations. This resulted in every member present voting for Clay, except one delegate who had no preference and was excused from voting.[69]   In accordance with the precedent established by the Antimasons, Clay was then unanimously nominated by acclamation. The chair was authorized to appoint a committee of seven to draft the customary address to the nation and of this body Alexander H. Everett was chairman.

Another convention precedent was established when each delegation was authorized to name one member of a notification committee which should apprise Clay of his nomination. The method of doing this was left to the committee's discretion, so they addressed him a letter and delegated a sub-

[67] Cf. Clay's letter, Niles' Register, vol. xli, p. 302, with his acceptance in ibid., p. 304. See also Andrew Stewart to McLean, November 24, 1831, McLean MSS.; Clay to Brooke, December 9, 1831, Clay, Correspondence, p. 321; Jackson to Van Buren, December 17, 1831, Van Buren MSS.; The Globe, December 15, 1831, excerpt from [Philadelphia] National Gazette.

[68] Niles' Register, vol. xli, p. 302.

[69] Ibid., pp. 302–303; Journal of the National Republican Convention.

committee of five to set out for Washington with it at once. The convention then adjourned until the next day.[70]

The delegates, and the party as well, had heretofore apparently been so intent on nominating Clay for president that no one seems to have given any thought as to who should be second on the ticket, and there was no consensus of opinion in favor of anyone,[71] hence no nomination for vice-president was attempted immediately after the choice of Clay. The selection must have been made in caucus or consultation outside the convention, but there is no definite information as to this.

On Wednesday, after some minor business such as seating a few late-arriving delegates, the notification committee read Clay's brief letter of acceptance, which was received with great applause. A motion was then adopted to proceed with the vice-presidential nominations, and Boyd McNairy, the sole delegate from Tennessee, placed John Sergeant of Pennsylvania in nomination, but without making a speech. At this juncture Walter Jones of the District of Columbia delegation arose and made the first speech in national convention history seconding a nomination. There were no more nominations, and by the same method as had been used the day before Sergeant was unanimously nominated, and a committee of five was appointed by the chairman to notify him. The convention then appointed a finance committee to meet printing and incidental expenses, and another to wait on Carroll, who was unable to accept the invitation to visit the meeting, and ascertain a time when the convention could call on him in a body. Adjournment until next day then followed.[72]

On Thursday the convention provided for the further conduct of the campaign by recommending to the party in each

[70] Journal of the National Republican Convention; Niles' Register, vol. xli, p. 303.

[71] Niles' Register, vol. xli, pp. 304–305; Globe, December 15, 1831, excerpt from [Philadelphia] National Gazette.

[72] Niles' Register, vol. xli, p. 304; Journal of the National Republican Convention.

State to form a central corresponding committee, and to organize local committees in every county and town. It was nearly eleven months before the election would take place, too long an interval to pass without some further large demonstration by the party, hence it was felt necessary to stir up enthusiasm by another convention. Therefore a resolution was adopted recommending to the young men of the party to hold a national convention in Washington the first Monday in May, 1832. The committee's written notification to Sergeant and his acceptance were then read. After this the meeting took a recess until afternoon, when it reassembled at four o'clock and marched in a body to pay its respects to Charles Carroll.[73]

Friday, December 16, was the closing day. Its chief business was the reading and adoption of the address to the people. This document in substance was more nearly akin to the platform of to-day than that adopted by the Antimasons. The latter had been more of a diatribe against the evils of Masonry than a statement of remedial measures for those evils, and contained next to nothing in the way of a constructive governmental policy. The National Republican address was mainly a criticism of Jackson's administration as contrasted with that of Adams, and a condemnation of its policy as to removals from office, the Indians, internal improvemments, and the Bank. It recommended as the panacea for all these ills, the election of Clay and Sergeant.[74]

There followed a resolution to print 10,000 copies of this address, and another urging the delegates " to promote among their constituents a zealous support of the principles of the national republican party and of the candidates named by this convention." [75] Next came the usual votes of thanks to committees and officers, and, after an address by Barbour, the convention adjourned, sine die.[76]

[73] Niles' Register, vol. xli, pp. 305–306.
[74] Ibid., pp. 306–312.
[75] Ibid., p. 306.
[76] Ibid., p. 306; Journal of the National Republican Convention.

The National Republican convention was not a nominating body in as genuine a sense as was either the Antimasonic or the Democratic convention. Its choice of a candidate was so certain before the convention was planned, that its nomination of Clay was more the act of a ratifying than that of a truly nominating body. At the same time there are certain points in convention practice for which this meeting of National Republicans deserves the credit above either of the other two conventions. Briefly stated they are: its nearer approach to a true key-note speech from its permanent chairman; the first nominating speech and the first seconding speech; the introduction of the oral vote by roll call; the present day form of the notification committee; and the greater party enthusiasm manifested in its proceedings.

CHAPTER IV

THE DEMOCRATS

Jackson had not been elected in 1828 by a definite political party, for that term implies a political group with definite constitutional principles and party organization. The following which had elected him had been, as a whole, united in but one purpose—to elect him president over Adams. Broadly speaking, his election was accomplished by his personal popularity, reinforced by the remnant of the old Republican party led by Van Buren, to which was joined the personal following of Calhoun. Each of these groups or factions, collectively known as "the friends of Jackson," had supported him from a different motive and expected a different result from the joint success. They may for convenience be styled the Western group, the Calhoun group, and the Crawford group.

The Western group, whose type he was, comprised the backbone of Jackson's strength. It embraced the bulk of the country's democracy, with most of its numbers west of the Alleghenies, in Pennsylvania, in western Virginia and North Carolina. Jackson was its idol and it was firmly convinced of his entire integrity in all things.[1] He knew these people thoroughly, understood better than any man of his time their likes and dislikes, and fully realized that most of his strength lay with them.[2] This group had enthusiastically supported him against what they regarded as a corrupt and unprincipled aristocracy[3] and confidently expected his election to introduce an era of reform and of government

---

[1] James Buchanan to McLean, June 11, 1829, McLean MSS.
[2] Van Buren, Autobiography, p. 253.
[3] W. B. Lewis to J. A. Hamilton, December 12, 1828, Van Buren MSS.

by the people,[4] however vague their ideas may have been as to the meaning of the latter phrase. In one respect this Western group was inferior to either of the other two. While it had many upright men like Hugh L. White, and many local politicians of some ability like Lewis and Kendall, of political leaders with a national reputation for acumen, education, and social standing, there was not one comparable to many in Calhoun's train.

The Calhoun group embraced the bulk of the party's aristocratic, educated and socially prominent men of national reputation, both in Congress and in politics. Numerically it was the smallest of the three groups; in the weight of its leaders' influence in the party it was the strongest. It numbered among these leaders Calhoun himself, James Hamilton, Jr., Robert Y. Hayne, George M. Dallas, Samuel D. Ingham, John Branch and John McP. Berrien. It was the dominant political force in South Carolina, with considerable strength in Alabama, Mississippi, North Carolina and Pennsylvania. The culture, standing, and constitutional doctrines of its leaders likewise appealed strongly to Virginia. Led by Calhoun, it had supported Jackson mainly for the advantage which, through its leader, it expected to derive from such support.[5] As the campaign had progressed and opposition to the tariff had grown stronger, the rank and file of the faction, especially in South Carolina, became more and more actuated by dislike of Adams' nationalism and by the hope that Jackson's indefinite views on tariff and internal improvements would develop in favor of their particularism.

This strict construction sentiment and consequent dislike of Adams had been the factor which had enabled Van Buren to reestablish the Virginia-New York Alliance and to swing those States into the Jackson column. The bulk of the

---

[4] Jackson to Van Buren, March 31, 1829, Jackson MSS.; Benton, Thirty Years' View, vol. i, p. 111.
[5] Adams, Memoirs, vol. viii, pp. 506–507.

Crawford group was essentially strict constructionist in its principles and had made a choice between what it regarded as the lesser of two evils in supporting Jackson. It looked to Van Buren as its political leader, and it was his leadership, backed by Regency and Junto, which had insured success. It expected therefore of Jackson a cabinet of able men and a policy for which strict construction would be the basis. It outnumbered the Calhoun group, being in control of New York, Virginia, Georgia and North Carolina, but Van Buren aside, could not compare with the Calhoun group in number of nationally prominent political leaders.

On account of Van Buren's substantial contribution to Jackson's success, the consensus of opinion in both the Western and Crawford groups of Jacksonians had been for six months before the election that to him was due the chief position in the new cabinet, and that he would receive it.[6] That Calhoun had supported Jackson, with the expectation of succeeding him as president, there is no doubt.[7] Furthermore, Jackson's advocacy of one-term presidential tenure [8] would naturally confirm Calhoun in the belief that the President would retire at the end of four years. In addition, Jackson's frail health in 1829 made it doubtful if he would survive four years,[9] far less undergo the turmoil of another campaign. For these reasons as well as for the important part the leaders of his group had played in supporting Jackson, Calhoun expected not only to be the heir apparent, but also to have several of his friends in the cabinet.[10] According to Benton and Van Buren,[11] Jackson regarded Calhoun at this time with favor as his successor.

It was these cabinet selections which gave rise to the first traces of the intra-party contest for the succession. The

---

[6] Hammond, vol. ii, pp. 282–283; Ritchie to Van Buren, March 11, 1828, January 31, 1829; Lewis to Van Buren, December 12, 1828, Van Buren MSS.; Van Buren, Autobiography, pp. 224, 229–231.
[7] Cf. Adams, Memoirs, vol. vi, pp. 506–507.
[8] Niles' Register, vol. xxix, p. 157.
[9] M. T. Simpson to McLean, March 1, 1829, McLean MSS.
[10] Van Buren, Autobiography, p. 341.
[11] Ibid., p. 410.

Western group of leaders felt that they had formed the basis of Jackson's success and were distinctly averse to seeing the Calhoun leaders compose the majority of the cabinet. Moreover, they had been closely in touch with Van Buren during the campaign; hence it was but natural that they should welcome the New Yorker as Secretary of State and as a possible ally. From the first of December, 1828, to the end of February, 1829, Washington was the scene of a preliminary skirmish between Calhoun partizans on the one hand and the Western group, aided by Van Buren's friends, on the other, over the cabinet personnel. Calhoun and Van Buren were not in the city during this time, but their respective friends were most active. Duff Green was openly referring to his patron, Calhoun, as the party's next candidate for president, and intimations and rumors were set on foot by others to discourage Van Buren from accepting the State Department.[12] The Western group of Jacksonians, led by White, Eaton, Moore and Bradley, espoused Van Buren's cause, and he was represented by his friends James A. Hamilton and G. C. Verplanck. Their efforts were mainly directed toward counteracting rumors and reports hostile to Van Buren. This marks the beginning of the struggle for supremacy and the succession within the Democratic party between the Calhoun group on the one side and the Van Buren on the other, the latter including Jackson's Western following.

Jackson himself settled the cabinet question and to no one's liking but his own.[13] To Van Buren went the chief place. Jackson, bent on having one personal friend in the cabinet, gave the War Department to John H. Eaton, and eventually made another Westerner, William T. Barry, Post-Master General. Calhoun's friend, Samuel D. Ingham of Pennsylvania, received the Treasury Department, another

---

[12] Gulian C. Verplanck to Van Buren, December 6, 1828, December 30, 1828, Van Buren MSS.

[13] J. A. Hamilton, Reminiscences, pp. 89–101.

friend, John Branch of North Carolina, the Navy Department, and still another, John M. Berrien of Georgia, the Legal Department.[14] The one point upon which this cabinet could agree was aversion to Clay; there was no other harmonizing factor; and there was a distinct coolness between Van Buren and Berrien from the outset.[15] All the elements for a contest for supremacy were present; Van Buren, Eaton and Barry against the three Calhoun men, with Jackson's sympathy inclined toward the former. But it was Jackson's choice and nothing would induce him to change it. It was his first positive assertion of himself as the de facto head of the party.

Jackson seems to have been ignorant of, or else to have deliberately ignored, the possibilities of antagonism between these two cabinet groups. Unless harmony could be speedily developed between the two factions, an open break between their respective leaders, Calhoun and Van Buren, would be merely a matter of time. The President of course would be the determining factor. To the side he favored would go the prize, the support of his tremendous popularity and influence in the West exerted in behalf of his chosen successor.

Another factor, at first unnoticed, but destined to figure prominently in determining the outcome of the Calhoun-Van Buren contest, was the "Kitchen" or "Back-stairs Cabinet." All his past life Jackson had acted on his own judgment and responsibility in cardinal matters. As a general he had called few military councils. As President he seldom called cabinet meetings.[16] His opinion once formed was unshakable, but he did not usually resort to snap judgment. When he wanted advice he preferred to discuss the matter in hand with friends. There were several of these outside the official cabinet, in particular William B. Lewis,

[14] J. A. Hamilton to Van Buren, February 21, 27, March 6, 1829, Van Buren MSS.

[15] Van Buren, Autobiography, pp. 213–216.

[16] Niles' Register, vol. xxxvi, p. 317; Adams, Memoirs, vol. viii, p. 477.

his close friend for years, Amos Kendall, a Kentucky editor who had worked hard for him. Isaac Hill who had done likewise in New Hampshire, and Duff Green, editor of the Telegraph. Of these, Lewis was a member of his household and, like Kendall and Hill, was appointed to a position in the Treasury. These several friends, together with Eaton and Van Buren, were privileged to call upon him at almost any hour of day or night. This group was known as the "Kitchen Cabinet," and Jackson advised with its members much more than he did with the heads of the departments. A fact significant for Calhoun's future was that, excepting Duff Green whose membership was short, he had not a single warm friend in this body, and moreover its whole personnel was drawn from the most democratic and mainly from the western wing of the party. It would, therefore, from the outset, favor Van Buren against Calhoun and work against the latter and his friends.

Three months before Jackson's inauguration another force came into being which was to play a prominent part in promoting hostilities between the Van Buren and Calhoun groups—Mrs. Eaton. The daughter of a Washington tavern-keeper, physically attractive, of dubious reputation and little culture, she had married a dissolute navy purser, Timberlake by name, who later committed suicide. Common report linked her name with Eaton's in a manner not wholly creditable, even after her marriage to Timberlake. With Jackson's approval Eaton married this woman January 1, 1829.[17]

As soon as it was known that Eaton would be in the cabinet, an outcry arose from social Washington at the prospect of associating with his wife. Mrs. Calhoun was among the foremost in Washington society and Mesdames Ingham, Branch and Berrien were likewise prominent. On the other hand Jackson and Van Buren were widowers, and Barry sided with them. Mrs. Calhoun and the other social leaders

---

[17] Cambreleng to Van Buren, quoted in Parton, vol. iii, p. 185.

absolutely and persistently refused to associate with Mrs. Eaton, deliberately ignoring her when no other resource was available. Van Buren was attentive and polite to Mrs. Eaton. He and the British and Russian ministers, Vaughn and Krudener, single men like himself, and with whom he was on excellent terms, united with him and the President in a vain attempt to force Mrs. Eaton on society. It was perhaps the only contest in Jackson's career from which he did not emerge victor. Almost alone he sincerely believed in and strongly maintained with every available resource the lady's entire innocence.[18] It was to no avail, and the lady in question soon ceased attending social functions. Van Buren's attitude toward Mrs. Eaton, his able handling of the State Department, together with his amiable and conciliatory disposition greatly endeared him to Jackson, and gave the latter a very high opinion of the New Yorker's ability and talents.[19] Van Buren in return cordially and sincerely reciprocated these sentiments.[20] On the other hand, the refusal of the families of Calhoun and the three secretaries to associate with Mrs. Eaton in defiance of Jackson's wishes did not operate very favorably upon the President's opinion of these gentlemen.

The Eaton scandal was under way before Van Buren reached Washington in 1829, so of course he did not instigate it, nor is there any evidence connecting either him or Calhoun directly with utilizing the affair to advantage. However, Calhoun could not but view Van Buren's rise in Jackson's favor with alarm, and the New Yorker could not have been oblivious to the fact that attentions to Mrs. Eaton were highly pleasing to the President. In addition to this, the Van Buren group—the leaders of Jackson's western following, including the "Kitchen Cabinet," and the New Yorker's supporters of the former Crawford faction—were

[18] Parton, Life of Jackson, vol. iii, pp. 184–205; Bassett, Life of Jackson, vol. ii, pp. 458–474.
[19] Jackson to Hugh L. White, April 9, 1831, Jackson MSS.
[20] Van Buren, Autobiography, pp. 232, 345.

bent on utilizing the Eaton affair to secure Calhoun's downfall as heir apparent. Such being the case, it is not surprising that all efforts to quiet the scandal failed, that the affair dragged on through 1830, and that already by the end of 1829, according to a contemporary, the first officers of the government had divided into two hostile parties on the question of the proper treatment of Mrs. Eaton—Calhoun, Ingham, Branch and Berrien on one side, the President, Van Buren, Eaton and Barry on the other.[21] More serious for Calhoun still, relations between him and the President were seriously strained.[22]

In January, 1830, there occurred in the Senate the great Hayne-Webster debate on the theory of the Union, involving the main principles of States' Rights, and hinting at the principle of nullification. In this debate it was generally believed that Hayne was voicing the sentiments and opinions of Calhoun,[23] which fact did not at all raise Calhoun in Jackson's estimation. Since the Van Buren group had the President's private ear and most of his confidence, it is not surprising that warnings came to Jackson that Calhoun's friends were working secretly in Pennsylvania to undermine the President in order to limit him to one term. These warnings in the form of letters further asked why the President continued to maintain a plotter like Ingham in his cabinet.[24] On the heels of these warnings occurred the Jefferson anniversary dinner, April 13, 1830. This brought matters to a head. At this dinner Calhoun's entire committal to nullification became so fully apparent that from that moment his already slender chances for endorsement by Jackson as his successor vanished forever, as well as all his remaining chances of support from Pennsylvania.[25]

21 Mrs. M. B. Smith, The First Forty Years of Washington Society (Hunt, Ed.), p. 310.
22 Van Buren, Autobiography, p. 323.
23 Benton, Thirty Years' View, vol. i, p. 138.
24 Ross Wilkins to General Bernard, April 3, 1830; H. Petriken to Jackson, April 2, 1830, Jackson MSS.
25 Simpson to McLean, April 30, 1830; R. Ruggles to McLean, May 5, 1830, McLean MSS.

Calhoun had played into his enemies' hands, first in the Eaton affair, second indirectly through Hayne's sentiments in the debate with Webster, and lastly by his emergence at the Jefferson dinner into open accord with the nullificationists. This last ruined irreparably any remaining chance for support from Pennsylvania and New England should he bolt the Democratic party, and all three operated to intensify Jackson's growing dislike for him.

During all this time Calhoun's enemies held their deadliest weapon against him in reserve. When he was Secretary of War under Monroe, the Seminole War occurred, and Jackson, who pursued the Indians into Florida, had committed serious acts of indiscretion. In a cabinet meeting Calhoun expressed himself in favor of reprimanding or punishing Jackson in some way for exceeding his instructions. Of this fact Jackson still remained entirely ignorant, but Crawford of Georgia was fully informed and hated Calhoun cordially. Moreover two of the Georgian's former supporters and friends, now in the Jackson party, James A. Hamilton and John Forsyth, had learned of the matter from Crawford early in 1828, and the evidence was contained in a letter written to Hamilton by Forsyth after an interview with Crawford.[26] Hamilton was an intimate friend of Van Buren. He revealed this letter to Lewis in 1829.[27]

In November, 1829, Eaton and Lewis informed Jackson of the existence of this letter and he at once demanded it.[28] Forsyth was due in Washington as Senator from Georgia shortly, and thither came Hamilton also. After a conference with Jackson it was agreed that Forsyth should write Crawford for more authoritative and corroborative evidence. This was early in December, 1829. For some unknown reason Forsyth did not write Crawford until the sixteenth of

---

[26] Niles' Register, vol. xl, p. 45.
[27] Van Buren, Autobiography, pp. 368-373; Parton, Life of Jackson, vol. iii, pp. 310-320.
[28] Lewis' statement, given in Parton, vol. iii, pp. 323-324.

the following April,[29] three days after the Jefferson dinner had placed Jackson squarely and openly at odds with Calhoun as to nullification. This circumstance looks as if the delay had been deliberate, as if awaiting an especially favorable opportunity for placing in Jackson's hands such a weapon for Calhoun's undoing.

Crawford replied to Forsyth on April 30, 1830, with a letter in which he stated that Calhoun had in Monroe's cabinet advocated that "Jackson should be punished in some form, or reprimanded in some form."[30] On May 12, 1830, Forsyth delivered his letter to Jackson who enclosed it next day to Calhoun, with a short but pointed request to be informed if it was true.[31] Calhoun replied at once stating that he would deal with the matter more at length in a few days and expressing his indignation at it as the culmination of "the secret and mysterious attempts which have been making, by false insinuations, for years, for political purposes, to injure my character."[32]

Calhoun had not been guilty of duplicity toward Jackson. Since his opinion, expressed in cabinet meeting and so under restriction of secrecy, was not adopted, it made no difference, and he was under no obligation to reveal it, quite the contrary in fact. His best course now would have been to assume high ground, to refuse to disclose cabinet secrets and so let the matter rest. He was betrayed by an apparent desire to stand well with Jackson, and on May 29, 1830, replied at prodigious length,[33] practically admitted that the charge was true, attempted to justify himself, and ascribed

---

[29] For Crawford's and Forsyth's letters, see Niles' Register, vol. xl, p. 12.

[30] Crawford to Forsyth, April 30, 1830, Niles' Register, vol. xl, p. 12.

[31] Van Buren, Autobiography, p. 374; Jackson to Calhoun, May 13, 1830, Jackson MSS.

[32] Calhoun to Jackson, May 13, 1830, Niles' Register, vol. xl, p. 12.

[33] Calhoun to Jackson, May 29, 1830, Jackson MSS. This letter is 48 pages long.

the whole affair to machinations of political enemies. Jackson forthwith replied that he had asked for no justification of Calhoun's motives but merely to know if the charge was true, and that, as Calhoun admitted having acted insincerely, "no further communication with you on this subject is necessary." [34]

Calhoun's political undoing was complete. Before him lay a choice of two courses. He could either go to the enemy and follow Clay's leadership, a move which meant political suicide in the South, or else remain in the party under the scowl of Jackson and attempt to force himself upon the latter as his successor and the party's future leader by crushing every competitor. He decided upon the second alternative.

Despite Van Buren's refusal to have anything to do with the controversy between Jackson and Calhoun,[35] the latter firmly believed that Van Buren was at the bottom of the attack on him.[36] He had been of this opinion for about six months before the break with Jackson, and his friends had been fighting hard against the Van Buren group during that time.[37] Calhoun's great difficulty in the struggle was stated by Webster thus: "Calhoun is forming a party against Van Buren, and as the President is supposed to be Van Buren's man, the Vice-President has great difficulty to separate his opposition to Van Buren from opposition to the President." [38] The breach between Calhoun and Jackson was not known to the public at the time—May, 1830. It was certain to leak out in the course of some months, however, and Calhoun and his friends resolved to be prepared against that day. Accordingly, with Duff Green as the agent, they began form-

---

[34] Jackson to Calhoun, May 29, 1830, Niles' Register, vol. xl, p. 17.
[35] Van Buren, Autobiography, p. 376; Parton, Life of Jackson, vol. iii, pp. 326–327.
[36] Calhoun, Correspondence, Annual Report of the American Historical Association for 1899 (J. F. Jameson, Ed.), vol. ii, pp. 289–291.
[37] Webster, Correspondence, vol. i, p. 483.
[38] Ibid., p. 488.

ing a plan whose success would not only demolish Van Buren politically, but would also push Jackson aside as party leader and as candidate for reelection.

Duff Green's Telegraph, the party's official newspaper, had been consistently loyal to Calhoun. Indeed, since the beginning of the administration its inclination had been more toward Calhoun than toward Jackson, but this it had kept for the most part within bounds. Green had become dissatisfied three months after Jackson was inaugurated, because he was not given a larger share of the public printing, of which he already did a large part.[39] As the Van Buren group grew in strength and in favor with Jackson, " General Duff " became more and more hostile to it and correspondingly ardent for Calhoun.[40] By the first of 1830, Green had become so distasteful to the West as party editor, that there were some in that section in favor of his removal.[41] In the spring and early summer of 1830, he began to differ with the administration's friends as to the value of the United States Bank. This drew a recommendation to Jackson from James A. Hamilton in New York to the effect that the administration " should change its *official organ*." [42] Between this date and the end of the year, Green and the Calhoun men were at work on their plan for achieving a complete victory.

The plan was, in brief, to acquire in each State the control of the party's leading newspapers and to place them in charge of Democrats friendly to Calhoun. This being effected, the Telegraph would startle the country by publishing the news of the rupture between the President and Calhoun, ascribe it to the intrigues of Van Buren, and publish the Jackson-Calhoun correspondence as proof. The controlled presses were then to take it up, openly to side with Calhoun, and the resulting outcry against Van Buren, it was

---

[39] Simpson to McLean, June 9, 1829, McLean MSS.; Benton, vol. i, p. 129.

[40] Simpson to McLean, October 11, 1829, McLean MSS.

[41] J. P. Taylor to McLean, January 31, 1830, McLean MSS.

[42] Hamilton to Jackson, July 29, 1830, Jackson MSS.

expected, would be so great that not even Jackson's popularity would save the situation. This, it was hoped, would ruin Van Buren politically, and perhaps prevent Jackson from becoming a candidate for reelection. Calhoun, it should be stated, had during this time been making every effort to collect proof of his entire blamelessness and of Van Buren's responsibility for the rupture with Jackson. His long letter to Jackson of May 29, 1830, had been written with an eye to future publication, and he had labored hard to show that the break was the result of "a political maneuver in which the design is that you [Jackson] should be the instrument and myself the victim, but in which the real actors are carefully concealed." [43] During the remainder of 1830, he wrote Monroe and the members of his cabinet seeking documentary evidence that Jackson had exceeded his orders in the Florida campaign.[44] This was to show the rectitude of his own course toward Jackson in 1818.

In the course of the attempt to gain control of newspapers, Duff Green had revealed the plan to Gideon Welles, then editor of the Jackson paper at Hartford, Connecticut,[45] and also to J. M. Duncanson, one of the administration's job printers in Washington, whose establishment he offered to buy and then to vest in him the editorship of the Frankfort [Kentucky] Argus.[46] Both of these gentlemen revealed the plot to Van Buren and Jackson. This scheme, inklings of which had doubtless reached the administration in the fall of 1830, together with Duff Green's other shortcomings, resulted in the elimination of the Telegraph as the party organ. A friend and former co-editor of Kendall's, Francis P. Blair, was called to Washington from Kentucky, and with the aid and patronage of the administration established The Globe, whose first issue appeared about the first of Decem-

---

[43] Calhoun to Jackson, May 29, 1830, Jackson MSS.; Niles' Register, vol. xl, p. 16.
[44] Niles' Register, vol. xl, pp. 23-24.
[45] Welles to Van Buren, December 27, 1830, Van Buren MSS.
[46] Benton, vol. i, pp. 128-129.

ber, 1830.[47] Administration papers then proclaimed far and wide that the Telegraph no longer enjoyed the administration's confidence, and that henceforth The Globe would function in that capacity. Thus Duff Green was placed in the same category as Calhoun, completely discredited with the bulk of the party but nominally still a member of it. By this means the administration fortified itself for its next passage at arms with Calhoun.

By the end of November, 1830, the rupture between Jackson and Calhoun was beginning to be known and references to its cause, often contradictory, were appearing in the papers.[48] Although, for all his efforts, Calhoun had not been able to trace the movement against him to Van Buren direct, he believed that the time was about ripe to expose the whole matter in detail and that to do so would blast Van Buren politically.[49] Inasmuch as many prominent members of the party feared that open rupture would distract and weaken it, attempts at reconciliation were made by mutual friends of the President and Vice-President. These attempts proved fruitless.

The Telegraph, on February 15, 1831, proceeded to prepare the way for the revelation by publishing extracts from certain newspapers to give the impression that Van Buren would come out for president if Jackson declined to run.[50] On the 17th, Green published the entire correspondence.[51] It was a bad move, for it savored too much of an attack on Jackson and the latter's friends rallied to him and Van Buren. The administration papers, led by The Globe, blazed forth against Calhoun immediately, denounced the publication of the correspondence as " wholly uncalled for " and as " a firebrand wantonly thrown into the Republican party," for

[47] Richards to McLean, December 1, 1830, McLean MSS.
[48] Ibid., Van Buren, Autobiography, p. 376.
[49] Calhoun, Correspondence, pp. 279–283.
[50] Telegraph, February 15, 1831.
[51] Ibid., February 17, 22, 1831; Niles' Register, vol. xl, pp. 11–24

which " Calhoun will be held responsible." [52] To this the Calhoun papers, especially in Virginia and South Carolina, retorted by accusing Van Buren of bringing about the break by means of political trickery in order to further his own interests.[53] There was, however, no general rising of the press in favor of Calhoun; that plan had been frustrated by the prompt and timely elimination of the Telegraph as the party newspaper, and by the hold which Jackson had on the vast majority of his party.

From this time there was open war between the main part of the party led by Jackson and such insurgents as Calhoun could enlist. The former struggle between the Van Buren and Calhoun groups over the succession entered its second phase with the open break between Calhoun and the President. This break was a distinct triumph for the Van Buren element since it aligned the weight of Jackson's strength with them. As Calhoun could not easily leave the party, the contest was now resolved into an effort by him, with any assistance he could obtain, to defeat Van Buren in 1832 for either president or vice-president.

This struggle between the Calhoun and Van Buren factions, resulting in the former's insurgency, was directly responsible for Jackson's determination to be a candidate for reelection, if the people appeared to desire it. Previous to his election and again in both his first and second messages to Congress he had recommended a limitation of the presidential tenure to one term.[54] He seems to have preferred sincerely a peaceful retirement to the Hermitage as soon as compatible with the duties which he believed the people desired him to perform.[55] His break with Calhoun and the opinion he had formed of the latter's duplicity and

---

[52] Globe, February 21, 1831.
[53] Niles' Register, vol. xl, pp. 70-72.
[54] Richardson, Messages and Papers of the Presidents, vol. ii, pp. 448, 518-519.
[55] Jackson to Van Buren, August 8, September 5, 18, 1831, Van Buren MSS.

attitude as to nullification, together with his admiration and friendship for Van Buren were prominent factors in his decision to stand for reelection. He was furthermore influenced by the fact that his party was not yet a completely united political unit, and another campaign would be necessary to accomplish such a result and to enable him to designate his successor. An additional incentive was the fact that Calhoun could probably defeat Van Buren for the party's presidential nomination, as the latter was not at all widely popular. This being the case, quite naturally the Van Buren group spared no pains to impress upon Jackson the people's desire that he should stand for reelection. Over and above all this, Jackson had his heart set on the payment of the national debt as a triumph of an economical policy, and had also begun a struggle with the Bank of the United States, on whose overthrow he believed the nation's future was largely dependent. He was the more ready for a second campaign since the National Republicans led by Clay were attacking his measures past and present furiously, and the old soldier's " determination never to be driven by my enemies " made a withdrawal under fire repugnant to him.[56]

The Van Buren group were not ignorant of the danger of attempting to combat Calhoun for the presidency in 1832, even with Jackson's aid, and hence neglected no precautions to convince the "Old Hero" that the people wanted him for president again.[57] Early in 1830 the New York Courier and Enquirer began breaking ground for Jackson.[58] Working through the editor of the party paper at Harrisburg, the "Kitchen Cabinet" drew up a letter to Jackson signed by sixty-eight members of the Pennsylvania legislature, requesting the President to stand for reelection.[59] This was but the beginning. On March 31, 1830, the Jackson members of that legislature, after a sharp contest with the Cal-

[56] Ibid., September 18, 1831.
[57] Clay, Correspondence, pp. 259-260, 262-263.
[58] New York Courier and Enquirer, March 12, 15, 20, 1830.
[59] Parton, Life of Jackson, vol. iii, pp. 279-302.

houn faction in that body, carried resolutions endorsing the administration, and stating, "That . . . the unity and harmony of the great democratic party of the Union will be greatly promoted " by Jackson's reelection.[60]   The Regency-controlled legislature in New York followed suit April 13,[61] and thus, before Jackson broke with Calhoun in May, there was already considerable pressure upon the President to be again a candidate.   The action of the Democrats of the Pennsylvania and New York legislatures was followed by those of New Hampshire in June,[62] and of Alabama in December, 1830,[63] and in January, 1831, before the rupture with Calhoun was openly proclaimed, The Globe announced itself authorized to say that the President would not decline a second term.[64]

Jackson regarded Calhoun's publication of their correspondence in the light of an open defiance.   Once engaged in a cause he never stopped at half measures.   There were three of Calhoun's friends in the cabinet, of whose secret plotting, directed by Calhoun and Duff Green, Jackson was firmly convinced.[65]   By the first of 1831 he was ready for decisive action against these three, but caution was necessary.   The publication of the correspondence containing Calhoun's attempt to lay the blame for the break with Jackson at Van Buren's door had produced considerable excitement and indignation against the New Yorker in Virginia.   This was ominous, for Virginia at that time exerted a greater influence than any other State upon the general sentiment of the country.[66]   Van Buren was warned of

[60] Harrisburg Reporter, April 2, 1830, in Niles' Register, vol. xxxviii, pp. 169–170; H. Petriken to Jackson, April 2, 1830; Ross Wilkins to General Bernard, April 3, 1830, Jackson MSS.
[61] Niles' Register, vol. xl, p. 170.
[62] Ibid., vol. xxxviii, pp. 292–293.
[63] Ibid., vol. xxxix, p. 341.
[64] Ibid., p. 385; cf. also ibid., vol. xl, p. 127.
[65] C. I. Jack to ———, November 10, 1830; Jackson to Mrs. Emily Donelson, January 20, 1831, A. J. Donelson MSS.; Jackson to Overton, December 31, 1830, Jackson MSS.
[66] Van Buren, Autobiography, p. 385.

danger by his friend Ritchie [67] just after the correspondence
had been published. A fortnight later another friend, W. S.
Archer, a Congressman, wrote from Richmond in great alarm
that Van Buren was widely regarded as the prime mover in
the plot to overturn Calhoun in the administration's confidence, that there was much sympathy for Calhoun, that
the administration was highly unpopular and that nothing
could restore it except a thorough reorganization of the
cabinet, including Van Buren's resignation.[68]

In this crisis, Van Buren resolved upon a master stroke—
to resign from the cabinet himself and if possible to draw
Eaton into a like course. This would enable Jackson to remove the Calhoun members and would go far toward con-
tradicting the impression that Van Buren himself had caused
the rupture to further his own ambition. The difficulty was
to win over Jackson himself, as his loyalty to Van Buren
and Eaton would operate powerfully against a course which
to him would at first appear tantamount to quitting under
fire from the enemy. At last, however, Van Buren succeeded in convincing Jackson of the advisability of his
resignation. The President would not hear of his retiring
to private life lest the enemy regard it as a victory, and insisted that the secretary take the mission to England instead. Eaton's name was not first mentioned. However,
as the plan was discussed between Jackson, Van Buren,
Eaton, Lewis and Barry, the drift of the conversation was
doubtless so much in that direction that Eaton finally announced that he also would resign.[69]

Thus the obstacle was surmounted, and in April the resig-
nations were published, Ingham, Branch and Berrien being
forced to resign by Jackson. Edward Livingston became
the new Secretary of State, Van Buren replaced Louis

---

[67] Ritchie to Van Buren, February 21, 1831, Van Buren MSS.;
Van Buren, Autobiography, pp. 385–386.
[68] W. S. Archer to Van Buren, March 12, 1831, Van Buren MSS.
[69] For complete account of the cabinet break-up, see Van Buren,
Autobiography, pp. 402–408.

McLane in London and the latter received the Treasury Department. Cass was made Secretary of War, Levi Woodbury Secretary of the Navy and Taney Attorney-General. Barry was not removed as his place was not regarded as of sufficient importance. During this and the preceding months the " Kitchen Cabinet " also underwent a change in personnel. Duff Green had long since been cast out and replaced by Blair. Lewis by opposing Jackson's Bank policy had weakened his former influence as to matters of policy and was limited mostly to party manipulation. Kendall and Hill, who agreed with Jackson as to the Bank, together with Blair, were now closest to the President. To these should be added Taney and Barry of the official cabinet. Indeed, with the new cabinet composing a harmonious whole, Jackson was less given to advising with the " Kitchen Cabinet " in cardinal matters of policy, but he depended more upon it for the actual management and wire-working necessary to the direction of the party as a political unit.

The cabinet reorganization marks another step in the solidification of the Democratic party under Jackson's undisputed leadership. The Maysville veto was the first step, and but one more now remained—the United States Bank veto—which will be noticed in a later chapter. This increase in the party's solidarity was reflected in the fall elections which so effectively sustained the administration that for the time being Calhoun's insurgent faction of the party almost disappeared, even in Virginia.[70] This result convinced the South Carolinian and his friends of the futility of attacking the administration and hence their efforts for some months to come were directed mainly against Van Buren as a vice-presidential possibility.

Van Buren's apparent self-abnegation had raised him still higher in Jackson's estimation. He sailed for London in August, 1831,[71] but still remained in close and direct com-

[70] John Campbell to Van Buren, October 4, 1831, Van Buren MSS.; Clay, Correspondence, pp. 322-323.
[71] Van Buren, Autobiography, p. 445.

munication with the President. He was not widely popular in the country, however, and not generally as well known as Calhoun. His reputation as a political manager, wire-worker and manipulator caused him to be widely disliked in Pennsylvania even among Jacksonians,[72] and so great was suspicion of him in Virginia that only his resignation from the cabinet had prevented the Calhoun faction from getting control of that State.[73] From Jackson's letters to him during the last half of 1831, it appears plainly that the President had fixed on Van Buren as his successor and had even considered resigning in the latter's favor if successfully reelected in 1832, provided the national debt and the Bank could be settled previously.[74] While these letters show that Jackson preferred Van Buren for vice-president,[75] he seems to have been neither confident of, nor determined upon, the gratification of this preference.[76] Indeed Van Buren's chances for the succession by way of the vice-presidency were far from good at this time. He had left the country without apprising his friends of any definite desire for the second office of the government.[77] and even the Richmond Junto was not inclined to favor him for it.[78] In addition to this, there were several other candidates in the field, all standing high in their respective States and in the party's councils, namely, Mahlon Dickerson of New Jersey, Philip Barbour of Virginia, William Wilkins and G. M. Dallas of Pennsylvania, Samuel Smith of Maryland and Richard M. Johnson of Kentucky.[79]

---

[72] "A Friend" to Van Buren, March 25, 1831, containing circular to the Democrats in Pennsylvania, Van Buren MSS.

[73] Archer to Van Buren, March 12, October 3, 1831, Van Buren MSS.

[74] Jackson to Van Buren, August 8, September 5, 18, 1831, Van Buren MSS.

[75] Cf. Van Buren, Autobiography, p. 506.

[76] Jackson to Van Buren, December 17, 1831, Van Buren MSS.

[77] J. W. Webb to Van Buren, December 31, 1831; Jackson to Van Buren, December 6, 1831, Van Buren MSS.

[78] Ritchie to Van Buren, April 30, 1831, Van Buren MSS.

[79] Webb to Van Buren, December 31, 1831; Walter Lowrie to Van Buren, January 27, 1832, Van Buren MSS.

Van Buren was not out of touch with the situation as his letters to Jackson and to his lieutenants Cambreleng, Marcy and Hamilton indicate, and his organization in New York had the situation in that State well in hand. He wrote Jackson on November 11, 1831, referring to the election in 1832, " The only point in the Union . . . which will require particular attention will be New York. My undivided attention will be directed to it . . . and it shall go hard, if we do not direct it to a safe and glorious result." [80] His most trusted lieutenant, a politician little inferior to himself, with whom he was in closest communication and most of whose letters he destroyed after reading,[81] was Churchill C. Cambreleng, Congressman from New York City. His care of Van Buren's interests and his political insight appear clearly from the following:

Some of your best friends . . . wish most sincerely, and I am among the number, that the senate would reject you! I know you will be annoyed at such a result—but it's the only thing that can remedy your error in going abroad—it's the only thing that can prevent the election in 1836 from going to the House. . . . Something striking—something to unite the party on a successor is absolutely necessary. . . . If you could but be rejected—you would return in triumph—we should have . . . the King, commons, and people against the Lords—You would be identified with the party and without a competitor . . . but they are too cunning to do you such a service. . . . I say again I wish they would.[82]

This very thing needed to unite the Democratic party on a vice-president as well as presumptive successor to Jackson occurred on January 25, 1832. Calhoun, smarting under past defeats, took the lead in joining forces with Clay and Webster in the Senate and defeated Van Buren's nomination as minister to England by one vote.[83] The whole proceeding was arranged so as to give Calhoun the pleasure of negativing what he fondly believed to be his rival's political

---

[80] Van Buren to Jackson, October 11, 1831, Van Buren MSS.
[81] Van Buren to Cambreleng, October 14, 1831, Van Buren MSS.
[82] Cambreleng to Van Buren, January 4, 1832, Van Buren MSS.
[83] Marcy to Van Buren, January 26, 1832, Van Buren MSS.; Van Buren, Autobiography, pp. 512, 520.

prospects as well as present occupation. The ostensible cause for this action was the instructions which Van Buren as Secretary of State had given to McLane to govern him in negotiating with England for opening the West Indies to American trade. The charges alleged were that these instructions lowered the dignity of the United States as a nation. There was nothing in them, and the country speedily recognized the action of the Senate as a political maneuver.[84]

Calhoun was delighted; he is alleged to have said on the occasion, " It will kill him, sir, kill him dead. He will never kick, sir, never kick." [85] No less pleased were Benton and other friends of Van Buren. The former said immediately the vote was announced, " You have broken a minister and elected a Vice-President," [86] and also, " I am now for Van Buren for Vice-President first and then I am for Van Buren for President." [87] Jackson on hearing the news flew into a towering rage and used language neither mild nor complimentary to the Senate.[88] Aside from his fondness for Van Buren, he regarded the rejection as a direct insult to himself,[89] and immediately began active steps looking to Van Buren's nomination at the Baltimore Convention in May.[90] In this course he had the cordial concurrence of the party leaders.[91]

No greater or more foolish political blunder was ever made by Calhoun. The results of the rejection did for Van Buren the one thing above all others likely to benefit him most at Calhoun's expense. The result of this political per-

[84] Benton, Thirty Years' View, vol. i, pp. 214-219; Van Buren, Autobiography, pp. 454-456, 510-513, 520-527.
[85] Benton, Thirty Years' View, vol. i, p. 219.
[86] Ibid., p. 215.
[87] Lowrie to Van Buren, January 27, 1832, Van Buren MSS.
[88] Ibid.
[89] Jackson to John Randolph, March 3, 1832, Jackson MSS.; A. J. Donelson to John Coffee, January 26, 1832, Donelson MSS.
[90] Jackson to Felix Grundy, February 4, 1832, Jackson MSS.; Richards to McLean, January 16, 1832, McLean MSS.
[91] John Forsyth to Van Buren, January 28, 1832; Elijah Hayward to Van Buren, January 30, 1832, Van Buren MSS.

secution upon the party at large was immediate. Richard M. Johnson of Kentucky, probably the leading candidate for vice-president, at once announced his withdrawal in Van Buren's favor.[92]   In New York it produced a veritable ferment.[93]   Resolutions of sympathy were sent to Van Buren, and the legislature voted resolutions of confidence in Van Buren and the administration, and of censure for Calhoun.[94] In Pennsylvania, where Van Buren was least popular, a temporary reaction in his favor resulted.[95]   In Virginia, so strong was the dislike of persecution, that sentiment swung strongly to Van Buren and the Junto at once began to utilize it.[96]   From Jackson's friends in Tennessee and Alabama came news of Van Buren's rise in popular estimation and pledges of support for him.[97]   In short, as Cambreleng wrote Van Buren, "the rejection . . . has made you twice as strong as you ever were at home and has made a party for you throughout the union."[98]

Van Buren was much surprised at his enemies' blunder. His political future was assured and it only remained for him to avoid mistakes. So careful was he that he did not even wish to appear to exploit the sentiment in his favor at home, and so took care not to arrive there until after the party convention at Baltimore.[99]   He contented himself with a trip to the continent and with a letter to his friends authorizing the use of his name for vice-president.[100]

---

[92] Blair to Van Buren, January 28, 1832, Van Buren MSS.; J. W. Webb to Nicholas Biddle, February 5, 1832, Biddle MSS.
[93] Hamilton to Van Buren, February 1, 1832, Van Buren MSS.
[94] In Van Buren MSS. dated January 31, and February 3, 1832.
[95] Simpson to McLean, February 2, 8, 1832, McLean MSS.
[96] Richard E. Parker to John Campbell, February 3, September 5, 1832; Andrew Stevenson to Ritchie, February 4, 1832, Van Buren MSS.
[97] William Carroll to Jackson, February 7, 1832; John Coffee to Jackson, February 24, 1832; Eaton to Jackson, March 22, 1832, Jackson MSS.
[98] Cambreleng to Van Buren, February 4, 1832, Van Buren MSS.
[99] Van Buren to John Van Buren, February 23, 1832, Van Buren MSS.
[100] Van Buren to Marcy, March 14, 1832, Van Buren MSS.

Calhoun and his followers speedily realized their blunder and set to work to counteract it. There was no hope of defeating Jackson, hence they made a virtue of necessity and professed to support him. At the same time they concentrated their efforts on the vice-presidential contest, hoping either to defeat Van Buren in the convention, or if that failed, to place another candidate in the field, intending by thus splitting the party's vote to prevent Van Buren from gaining an electoral majority, and so to relegate his chances of election to the tender mercies of the Senate.[101] Accordingly they insisted that as Jackson was not opposed to the tariff, it was only fair that Southern interests should be safe-guarded by the selection of an anti-tariff Southerner for second place on the party's ticket, and centered their efforts in Virginia, South Carolina and Alabama to procure the election of delegates who would support Philip P. Barbour of Virginia at Baltimore.[102] Their preference for Barbour was due to his States' Rights views, to his popularity in Virginia, to the fact that he was still in the administration's good graces,[103] to his liking for Calhoun, and also to the fact that the latter, now serving his second vice-presidential term, would not be favorably regarded for a third.[104]

Although Calhoun was now powerless in Pennsylvania, there was hope that that State would utterly refuse Van Buren, whom it associated with New York's political domination. The hope was well founded. Van Buren's enemies in the State were nearly as numerous as Jackson's admirers. Therefore, when on June 25, 1831,[105] the New Hampshire legislature recommended the Democratic convention of 1832 at Baltimore for the nomination of a vice-president, the

[101] Stevenson to Ritchie, February 4, 1832; F. P. Blair to Van Buren, January 28, 1832, Van Buren MSS.

[102] Blair to Van Buren, January 28, 1832, Van Buren MSS.

[103] Lewis to Van Buren, April 22, 1859, in Van Buren, Autobiography, p. 584.

[104] The Globe, July 6, 1831, reprint from New Hampshire Patriot.

[105] The Globe, July 6, 1831.

Pennsylvania Democrats feared that this had been engineered in Van Buren's interests, and bestirred themselves. Local meetings were held endorsing either Wilkins or Dallas, their Senators, for vice-presidential nominee with Jackson.[106] These meetings culminated in a state convention at Harrisburg, March 5, 1832. Its object was to nominate a vice-presidential candidate and so to forestall the Baltimore convention, or at least to influence its course.[107]

This Harrisburg convention was thoroughly representative of opinion in the State, and its delegates had been chosen in the same way as in 1824 and 1828; in addition most of them had been instructed for Wilkins or for Dallas. So close was the contest between these two for nomination on the ticket with Jackson, that, although the latter was almost unanimously supported for president, ten ballots were taken before Wilkins was chosen. Van Buren did not receive above four votes at any stage of the proceedings. To make assurance doubly sure against him, the convention then pledged its electoral ticket to vote for Dallas should Wilkins die before the election.[108]

The call for the Baltimore convention originated with the "Kitchen Cabinet," and as far as can be determined, though this body was friendly to Van Buren, its action was dictated rather by desire for party unity and harmony than by any design to force him upon the party as vice-president. With Calhoun openly eliminated by the spring of 1831, it required no gift of prophecy to tell that there would be many aspirants in the Democratic field for vice-presidential honors, hence the "Kitchen Cabinet"—now the directing power, under Jackson, of the party's politics—took the matter in hand. Lewis wrote to Kendall, who at the time—May 25, 1831—was visiting Isaac Hill, Senator-elect and political leader of New Hampshire. The letter gave the opinion of

---

[106] Ibid., July 14, 1831.
[107] Richards to McLean, March 17, 1832, McLean MSS.
[108] The Globe, March 8, 9, 1832; Niles' Register, vol. xlii, pp. 21, 72.

the party leaders in Washington that it was then too early
to bring out a vice-presidential candidate, mentioned Barbour and Dickerson as already in the field, and suggested
as the best means of uniting the party opinion on one man,
that a national convention be held in May, 1832, and that
such a step proposed by the New Hampshire legislature
would probably be concurred in by other States. It urged
Kendall to consider it and, if advisable, to suggest this step
to Hill.[109] In this letter Lewis merely took a leaf from the
enemies' books, since it was then generally known that both
Antimasons and National Republicans had fixed dates in
1831 for similar conventions, also at Baltimore.[110]

Kendall and Hill found Lewis' suggestion good and acted
accordingly.[111] Less than a month later a Democratic caucus
of the New Hampshire legislature recommended, " to their
republican brethren in other states, friendly to the reelection
of Andrew Jackson, to elect delegates equal to the number of
Electors of President in each state, to attend a general convention to be holden at Baltimore . . . on the third Monday of May, 1832; which convention shall have for its object the adoption of such measures as will best promote the
reelection of Andrew Jackson, and the nomination of a
candidate to be supported as Vice-President at the same election." [112] This The Globe approved and recommended to
the party throughout the country. It was endorsed by a
public meeting at Philadelphia July 11,[113] and subsequently
in various States. Between this time and the end of March,
1832, every State in the union except Virginia and Pennsylvania had appointed delegates.[114]

The method of appointing delegates varied in different
States. In New Hampshire they were appointed by legis-

[109] Lewis to Kendall, May 25, 1831, in Parton, Life of Jackson,
vol. iii, pp. 282-283. See also Van Buren, Autobiography, p. 584.
[110] Niles' Register, vol. xxxix, pp. 58, 91. Ibid.
[111] Van Buren, Autobiography, p. 584.
[112] The Globe, July 6, 1831, reprint from the New Hampshire
Patriot.
[113] Ibid., July 19, 1831.
[114] Ibid., January 3, 23, March 20, 22, 1832.

lative caucus.[115]   In North Carolina, Kentucky and Ohio they were appointed by state conventions.[116]   In Virginia the choice was made by local meetings of city and county.[117]   In Pennsylvania the bulk of the party, having made its vice-presidential nomination, would not appoint delegates to Baltimore; hence only a dozen self-appointed individuals, like Simon Cameron and George Kremer, attended in the capacity of delegates,[118] and there were few leaders from that State at the convention.   From other States party managers were out in force, Hill from New Hampshire, Overton and Eaton from Tennessee, Lucas from Ohio, Poinsett from South Carolina and several of both Regency and Junto.[119]

In a few of the States, there was something closely akin to instructed delegations.   Thus in New Jersey where the delegates were chosen by legislative caucus, they were " requested " to urge Mahlon Dickerson upon the convention for vice-president.[120]   In Alabama, where the Calhoun element had made strenuous efforts, the legislature instructed the delegates to vote for Barbour.[121]   In Kentucky the state convention instructed its delegates to vote for Richard M. Johnson.[122]

As to the size of delegations, the recommendation of the New Hampshire caucus, in initiating the convention movement, that each delegation should be equal to its State's quota in the electoral college, was strictly adhered to by about half of the States.[123]   In the other half, some States sent less and some more than this ratio.   Conspicuous among the

---

[115] Ibid., July 6, 1831.
[116] Ibid., January 3, 23, March 20, 1832.
[117] Richmond Enquirer, March 17, 20, 23, 1832.
[118] The Globe, May 29, 1832.
[119] Ibid.
[120] Ibid., March 20, 1832.
[121] F. P. Blair to Van Buren, January 28, 1832, Van Buren MSS.
[122] The Globe, January 3, 1832.
[123] Ibid., May 29, 1832, list of delegates by States. Summary of the Proceedings of Convention of Republican Delegates held at Baltimore, May, 1832, History Pamphlets, vol. 293, Johns Hopkins University Library.

latter were Virginia and New Jersey, whose delegates numbered 94 and 52 respectively. In every case, in the choice of delegates there was a general recognition of the fact that their sole functions were the nomination of a vice-president and the promotion of the ticket's success. Jackson's nomination was everywhere regarded as a *fait accompli*.

The Virginia situation needs some explanation. The leaders of the Junto desired to line up the State for Van Buren in spite of the formidable opposition supporting Barbour. In February, 1832, a state convention was called under Junto auspices. There was no difficulty in securing an endorsement of Jackson, but the fight over Van Buren was hotly contested and the Junto forces, seeing that the opposition was too strong, forced an adjournment.[124] A fortnight later a legislative caucus likewise failed to agree to support Van Buren and voted three to one against making any vice-presidential nomination. It also voted to leave the selection of delegates to Baltimore to the people.[125] The cities and counties therefore each chose delegates in numbers varying from one in the less important counties to half a dozen from the city and county of Richmond.[126]

Such were the origin and sources of " the Baltimore Democratic Republican Convention, appointed to nominate a candidate for Vice-President," [127] which assembled at the Athenaeum May 21, 1832. The total number of delegates was 334,[128] from every State except Missouri, whose delegates did not appear, and the average attendance was about 280.

The first day and a half was devoted to organization. Frederick A. Sumner of New Hampshire called the meeting to order and stated its objects as the harmonious choice of a vice-presidential candidate and the promotion of success at the coming election. After the election of temporary

---

[124] Ibid., March 20, 1832; Richmond Enquirer, March 17, 1832.
[125] Richmond Enquirer, March 17, 20, 23, 1832.
[126] The Globe, May 1, 29, 1832.
[127] Ibid., May 1, 1832.
[128] Ibid., May 29, 1832; Proceedings of the Convention.

officers, a committee of one from each State was appointed
to report to the convention a list of the delegates in attendance, a function closely analogous to that of the present-day
Credentials Committee. Following its report came a roll-
call of the delegates by States.[129]

These preliminaries accomplished, the convention authorized each state delegation to appoint one member of a committee whose duties would be to select permanent officers
and to prepare rules for the government of the convention.
Here we have the identical functions of the modern Committee on Permanent Organization and of that on Rules,
vested in one committee. This committee was the main-
spring of the convention, and the results of its labors are still
in force today. The meeting then adjourned until next
morning—Tuesday the 22nd.[130]

On the convention being called to order next day, the
organization-and-rules committee, with William R. King of
Alabama as chairman, reported. It recommended General
Robert Lucas, the chairman pro tempore, for the permanent
position, four vice-presidents—of whom Daniel of the Richmond Junto was the first—and three secretaries. Lucas
was then installed, and made a brief acknowledgment. This
completed the convention's organization.[131]

The committee then reported the rules. First and most
important of these was, " Resolved, That each state be entitled, in the nomination to be made of the candidate for the
vice-presidency, to a number of votes equal to the number to
which they will be entitled in the electoral colleges . . . and
that two-thirds of the whole number of the votes in the
convention shall be necessary to constitute a choice." [132]

---

[129] Ibid., May 23, 1832; Baltimore American, May 22, 1832; Proceedings of the Convention.

[130] The Globe, May 23, 1832; Baltimore American, May 22, 1832.
The Convention met on the 22nd and subsequently in the Univer-
salist Church, then on St. Paul Street just above Saratoga Street,
because the meeting was too large for the Athenaeum's capacity.

[131] The Baltimore American, May 23, 1832; The Globe, May 24,
1832; Proceedings of the Convention.

[132] Ibid.

King prefaced this resolution with a few remarks to the effect that the committee believed this to be the fairest apportionment of nominating votes. The two-thirds majority for nomination, he said, was desirable because a selection predicated upon it would indicate a more general concurrence of opinion, carry greater moral weight and be more favorably received by the country than one supported by a simple majority. Another important reason for its adoption was the presence of delegates from many States which would certainly vote against Jackson in the election.[133] There was some opposition and a motion was made to strike out the two-thirds clause; it failed to pass, however, and the rule was adopted unchanged, as it has remained ever since.[134]

The committee's next recommendation was almost equally important in convention history. It was " That in taking the vote, the majority of the delegates from each state designate the person by whom the votes for that state shall be cast," and that " in voting on the nomination for vice-president, the authorized person shall designate the name of the person to be voted for by the delegates from that state." [135] This was the first precedent for, and practice of, the Unit Rule. Its adoption was occasioned by two circumstances; first, the size of several delegations in proportion to the number of votes they were entitled to cast, and, second, certain state delegations were either instructed or expected by their constituents to vote for a particular candidate.[136] This rule, though adopted, was not rigidly enforced by this conven-

[133] Richmond Enquirer, May 29, 1832.
[134] Baltimore American, May 23, 1832; The Globe, May 24, 1832. In the Democratic Convention of 1836, and again in that of 1844, attempts were made to replace the " two-thirds " rule by a simple majority in making nominations. Both attempts failed. The decisive action of the convention of 1844 in refusing to replace the " two-thirds " rule by a simple majority resulted in the defeat of Van Buren for the nomination, and permanently established the " two-thirds " rule in Democratic convention practice (Edward Stanwood, History of Presidential Elections, pp. 116, 146-148.)
[135] The Globe, May 24, 1832.
[136] Richmond Enquirer, February 28, May 29, 1832; The Globe, May 29, 1832.

tion; some delegations, like that of Kentucky, observed it; others, notably Alabama, did not.[137]

The afternoon session this day brought the nomination. There were no nominating speeches.[138] The first ballot was the only one taken. On it Van Buren received 208 votes, about 40 more than the necessary two-thirds. Barbour received all those of Virginia and South Carolina, six each from North Carolina and Alabama and three from Maryland, a total of 49. Johnson received all those from Kentucky and Indiana and two from Illinois. Van Buren had all the rest and was declared duly nominated. The Virginia delegation, following a short recess, announced its concurrence in the nomination of Van Buren, in which course it was followed by those of Kentucky, Indiana and Alabama. The convention, doubtless encouraged by this, then adopted a resolution expressing its unanimous concurrence in recommending Van Buren to the country for the office of vice-president. This was followed by another resolution endorsing Jackson's character in highest terms and concurring in the various state nominations for president which he had received. This was the sole reference made to him during the convention. The president and vice-presidents were then appointed as a committee to notify Van Buren of his nomination, which they did at once by letter addressed to him at New York [139] since he had not yet returned from Europe. On recommendation from the organization-and-rules committee, a committee was then appointed to draft the usual address to the nation and the meeting adjourned to the next morning.[140]

At the session of Wednesday morning the address committee urged that in place of a general address to the people " it be recommended to the delegates to make such a report or address to their constituents as they might think proper."

137 Baltimore American, May 23, 1832; The Globe, May 24, 1832.
138 Ibid.
139 Letter is dated May 22, 1832, in Van Buren MSS.
140 Baltimore American, May 23, 1832; The Globe, May 24, 1832.

This effective substitute for the usual address issued by political meetings of that day, was adopted and nothing resembling a platform issued from this convention.[141]

The final business was the establishment of an effective campaign organization. This was done by authorizing each delegation to appoint a general correspondence committee for its State, and by the designation by the chairman of the convention of a general central committee to reside in the District of Columbia. Following this the usual votes of thanks to the meeting's officers were passed, and after resolving to wait upon Charles Carroll of Carrollton immediately thereafter, the convention adjourned sine die.[142]

One other transaction deserves notice. Sumner of New Hampshire, in his remarks at the initial session of the convention, in stating the motives which led his state legislature to call for a national convention, said that prominent among them was the desire to establish thus a precedent for future elections as a means of securing party harmony in making nominations.[143] Shortly before the convention adjourned, Simon Cameron of Pennsylvania offered a resolution to secure in future the convention mode of nominating candidates: "Resolved, That it is expedient and it is hereby recommended that such selections should be made by national conventions, composed of delegates to be selected by the democratic party of each state equal in number to the representatives of such state in . . . Congress . . . to assemble in the city of Baltimore the third Monday in May in every fourth year hereafter."[144] Some discussion arose and the resolution was withdrawn. The importance of the above speech and resolution lies in the fact that both clearly indicate, as was the case with the Antimasons, a recognition by the party of the need for larger, more far-reaching and better coordinated party machinery to effect presidential

---

[141] Ibid., May 24, 1832; Ibid., May 25, 1832.
[142] Ibid.
[143] The Globe, May 23, 1832.
[144] Baltimore American, May 24, 1832.

nominations and to promote the ticket's success. They further indicate a consciousness that the national nominating convention was best fitted to meet this need. Although Cameron withdrew his resolution, it is interesting to note that down to 1852, every subsequent Democratic convention was held in Baltimore, every one met in the presidential year in the month of May, and, excepting that of 1840, every one met on the third Monday of that month.[145]

The Democratic convention was in many respects the most important of the three held during this campaign, even though its object was only a vice-presidential nomination. In the first place it was larger than either of the others, both numerically and in the number of States represented. In the second place, representing a well-organized party, it sprang from a more definite party need, namely, the necessity for a harmonious selection from several vice-presidential aspirants, and was therefore less of an electioneering, propagandic measure than either of the others; hence it was most nearly of them all the true prototype of the nominating convention of today.

---

[145] Stanwood, History of Presidential Elections, pp. 115, 129, 145, 165, 180.

CHAPTER V

The Injection of the Bank into the Campaign

From a region where the banks were few, their operations of the " wildcat " variety, their paper money of dubious value, and their failures frequent, Andrew Jackson voiced his opinion of them when he said " I hate ragg, tagg banks and empty pockets."[1] From this it would appear that he regarded the paper money of banks and a deflated purse as cause and effect respectively, and specie as the only safe medium of exchange. Moreover he had been of this opinion ever since he had read of the South Sea Bubble.[2] More specific than this, he had opposed the founding of a branch of the United States Bank at Nashville, 1817–1818,[3] had expressed hostility to it in 1827,[4] and had been near introducing a passage against the parent Bank in his inaugural address.[5] Thus Jackson entered the presidency with a definite bias against the Bank as a financial institution. He further regarded it as unauthorized by the Constitution,[6] and at once began considering a substitute for it, and as early as May 2, 1829, wrote to Felix Grundy asking his views on the subject.[7] About the same time Nicholas Biddle, the able and autocratic president of the Bank, was desirous of winning Jackson's approval for that institution. He hoped to attain this

---

[1] Jackson to A. J. Donelson, August 19, 1820, Donelson MSS.
[2] Memorandum in Biddle's hand of a conversation with Jackson in November, 1829, Nicholas Biddle MSS.
[3] Bassett, Life of Andrew Jackson, vol. ii, p. 589; Catterall, The Second Bank of the United States, p. 183.
[4] Hamilton, Reminiscences, p. 69.
[5] Bassett, Life of Jackson, vol. ii, pp. 429–430; Catterall, p. 183.
[6] Biddle's memorandum of conversation with Jackson, November, 1829, Biddle MSS.
[7] Felix Grundy to Jackson, May 22, 1829, Jackson MSS.

object by offers to hand over to the Jacksonians the control of the Nashville branch and by convincing the President of the Bank's utility to the government in Jackson's pet policy, the payment of the last of the national debt by March 4, 1833.[8]

The institution of which Jackson disapproved had been chartered in 1816, primarily for the purpose of extricating the country from the financial debacle resulting from the War of 1812. After six years of struggle it came under Biddle's direction. Thanks to his able financial policy and careful attention to its affairs, the Bank soon thereafter began to prosper and by 1829 was entirely sound and flourishing, with its stock worth 122.[9] Of its capital of $35,000,000, one-fifth was subscribed by the United States, which likewise appointed one-fifth of the governing board of twenty-five directors, the remainder being chosen by the private stockholders. It was authorized by its charter to issue notes without restriction, provided it could redeem them in specie when presented or else pay interest on them at 12 per cent. These notes were receivable for government dues, a privilege accorded the notes of state banks only when they were redeemed in specie. In addition, the Bank enjoyed the use of the government's deposits without paying interest, but the Secretary of the Treasury could remove these at will provided he at once stated to Congress the reasons for so doing. Another power of great importance enabled the parent Bank at Philadelphia to establish branch offices of discount and deposit wherever it saw favorable openings. These branches were to be administered and governed by officers chosen by the central board of directors.[10]

In 1829 the Bank had twenty-four branches, one or more

---

[8] Thomas Cadwalader to Jackson, October 15, 1828, Jackson MSS.; William B. Lewis to Biddle, June 28, 1829, Biddle MSS.; Biddle to Asbury Dickins, May 19, 1829, Biddle's Letter Book among Biddle MSS.

[9] Niles' Register, vol. xxxvii, p. 359.

[10] Charter in United States Statutes at Large, vol. iii, pp. 266–277.

in every State except Delaware, Indiana and Illinois.[11] This widespread, highly centralized banking system was all-powerful in the country's banking operations. Its size and charter privileges gave it power over all state banks, no combination of which could hope to combat it successfully. By presenting for payment the quantities of state bank notes it received, it forced the latter to maintain reserves of coin adequate to support their note issues, and in this lay its chief advantage to the country.

At the close of 1829, more than one-fourth of its $28,000,000 of privately owned stock was in the hands of three hundred and eighty-three foreigners who had little influence in determining its policy. Of the remaining $20,800,000 in privately owned shares, over $16,000,000, or more than half the total amount of stock not owned by the United States government, was in the hands of a group of moneyed individuals, only eight hundred and twenty-two in number. None of these held less than $5,000 worth of stock, and more than half of them held $10,000 worth or more per capita. This group, if it so chose, had sufficient votes to control a decided majority of the twenty directors elected by the private stock holders. The remaining 2,780 American private stock holders held only a little more than $3,000,000 worth of shares.[12]

This centralization of financial power in the hands of a few, the size and strength of the Bank, its authority to extend its branches wherever it saw opportunity, its power to issue and control notes proportionate to the needs of the country's growing business, all together rendered it strongly monopolistic in character, beneficial to the nation, it is true, but with dangerous potentialities in the direction of centralization at local and state expense.

Owing to its power over their note issues, if for no other reason, the Bank was always disliked by the local state in-

---

[11] Catterall, Second Bank, p. 376.
[12] These facts are drawn from statement in Biddle's Letter Book, December 26, 1829.

stitutions. Since these latter were usually closely connected with local politics there was always opposition to the federal bank, particularly in the South and West. The growth of this opposition in the West was fostered greatly by the Bank's incidental profits from sales of land left on its hands as forfeited security resulting from the financial depression of 1819.[13] In the South the opposition naturally centered around the Bank's constitutional side.[14] This opposition to the institution had in the past found vent in attempts by the state legislatures to limit or destroy it. Here the Supreme Court intervened in the cases of McCulloh *vs.* Maryland and Osborn *vs.* The Bank of the United States, which made the Bank's position invulnerable for the duration of its charter. Although this status of the Bank had been generally acquiesced in several years prior to 1829, opposition to it was still latent in the hearts of the democratic masses of the West and those in the States' Rights men of the South.

With Jackson's accession, his democratic followers were not long in raising complaints against the Bank. These took the form of charges that in the late presidential contest the branches in Kentucky,[15] New Orleans,[16] and Portsmouth, New Hampshire.[17] had extended facilities to the supporters of Adams which had been denied to those of Jackson. The charges against the last of these involved Biddle in a correspondence with Ingham of the Treasury in the course of which Biddle practically informed the latter, on September 15, 1829, that it was none of the administration's business to enquire into the political opinions of the Bank's officers. This letter of Biddle's stirred Jackson's

---

[13] Benton, Abridgment of the Debates of Congress, vol. xi, p. 153; Bassett, Life of Jackson, vol. ii, p. 686.
[14] Judge John Catron to Donelson, December 31, 1829, Donelson MSS.; Niles' Register, vol. xxxvii, pp. 275, 367.
[15] McLean to Biddle, January 5, 1829, McLean MSS.
[16] M. L. Bevan to Biddle, October 21, 1829; Samuel Jaudon to Biddle, October 21, 1829, Biddle MSS.
[17] 22nd Cong., 1st sess., House Report No. 460, pp. 439–440.

antagonism. Among the latter's papers is an undated one in his own hand, headed " Extract from P. of the Bank." Immediately below this are copied the very lines of Biddle's letter of September 15, in which the latter had informed Ingham that the Bank directors " acknowledge not the slightest responsibility of any description whatsoever to the Secretary of the Treasury touching the political opinions and conduct of their officers,—that being a subject on which they . . . never desire to know the views of any administration." Immediately below these lines is written in Jackson's hand, " The Secretary must note ; & reply to that part of the P. . . . and relieve the executive from any interference with the Bank ; but remark, he reserves his constitutional powers to be exercised through Congress, to redress all grievances complained of by the people of the interference by the Branches with the local elections of the states, & all interference with party politicks, in every section of our country, where those complaints have reached the Executive." [18] Ingham replied in this tenor and at great length on October 5.[19]

Biddle sensed danger from the tone of Ingham's reply and renewed his efforts to gain the Executive's good will. He industriously investigated the charges against the branches of partiality and brought the results to Jackson's notice.[20] He kept in close touch with Lewis of the " Kitchen Cabinet " and consulted him about appointing friends of the administration to the directorates of various western and southwestern branches.[21] He advanced a plan whereby the administration might pay the last of the national debt on the anniversary of the battle of New Orleans in 1833.[22] He

[18] Undated memorandum in Jackson's hand, Jackson MSS., vol. lxxiv.

[19] Ingham-Biddle correspondence contained in 22nd Cong., 1st sess., H. Rept. No. 460, pp. 456–468; see especially pp. 460, 462, 466.

[20] Bevan to Biddle, October 21, 1829; Jaudon to Biddle, October 21, 1829, Biddle MSS.

[21] Biddle to Lewis, November 29, 1829 to May 8, 1830, in Biddle Letter Book.

[22] Ibid., November 15, 1829.

went to Washington about November 19, and conferred with Jackson in person.[23] In this interview Jackson expressed plainly his suspicion of all banks, that he believed Biddle's to be unconstitutional despite Marshall's opinion to the contrary, that he had every reason to be satisfied with the president and parent board of directors, and concluded by mentioning that he would mention the Bank's services in paying off the latest installment of the national debt in his approaching message to Congress.[24] Biddle, over prone to optimism, in which he was unduly encouraged by Lewis,[25] took this last remark of the President's to mean that he would speak in high terms of the Bank's value to the country.[26]

Mistaking thus Jackson's frank, courteous attitude toward him for approval of the Bank, Biddle and the institution's friends were vastly surprised and somewhat alarmed when the President, having mentioned the Bank's services in his message as he had said he would do, came out fairly and squarely against a renewal of the institution's charter on the ground that it was unconstitutional, inexpedient and had failed in "establishing a uniform and sound currency." He mentioned as a substitute for the present Bank one purely national in character, founded upon the government and revenues, but gave no details.[27] Biddle was so far from understanding Jackson's tenacity of purpose and party control that he regarded this part of the message as "an opinion of the President alone . . . a personal measure," and therefore far less dangerous than if it had been a cabinet or a party measure.[28]

[23] Biddle to General Sam Smith, January 2, 1830, Letter Book.
[24] Memorandum in Biddle's hand of conversation with Jackson, Biddle MSS.
[25] Lewis to Biddle, November 5, 11, 1829, Biddle MSS.
[26] Biddle to Sam Smith, January 2, 1830; to Alexander Hamilton, December 9, 10, 1829, Letter Book.
[27] Richardson, Messages and Papers, vol. ii, pp. 451, 462.
[28] Biddle to George Hoffman, December 15, 1829; to Sam Smith, January 2, 1830, Biddle MSS.

Biddle was wholly wrong in his belief, as events soon began to demonstrate, that this initial attack was an unsupported opinion of the President alone. As soon as the message reached New York the Bank's stock fell from 125¾ to 120.[29] On December 15 the South Carolina legislature began considering a resolution instructing its congressional delegation to oppose the rechartering of the Bank.[30] The opinion of the Western democracy on the subject was voiced by Judge John Catron, Chief Justice of the Tennessee Supreme Court. He heartily approved of Jackson's attack on the money monopoly which he declared was contrary to the interests of " the Southern & Western people," was sapping " the sound actions of our state governments . . . as well as those of the Fedrl. Govt. by controlling the elective franchise by the use of money." He added further that the preventing of rechartering it " *must be,* the rallying point of party; a warfare in which there can be no neutrality. . . . From the day Jackson was elected . . . I have believed this question, would here, & in Kentucky, destroy Mr. Clay's power if fully raised. . . . The message has *settled* the question." [31] To the same effect wrote also Jackson's friend and neighbor, Alfred Balch.[32]

Jackson's assertion that the Bank had failed in establishing a sound currency Biddle regarded as the most damaging. The latter therefore suggested to Sam Smith, Chairman of the Senate's finance committee, a friend of the Bank, that the best means of correcting this would be " for some Committee of Congress to negative the assumption that the currency is unsound." [33] That part of the message relative to the Bank had been referred in the House of Representatives to the Ways and Means Committee, of which George McDuffie, Calhoun's friend, was chairman. Know-

[29] Niles' Register, vol. xxxvii, p. 275.
[30] Ibid., pp. 275, 367.
[31] John Catron to Donelson, December 31, 1829, Donelson MSS.
[32] Alfred Balch to Jackson, January 7, 1830, Jackson MSS.
[33] Biddle to Sam Smith, January 2, 1830, Letter Book.

ing this, Biddle wrote Joseph Hemphill, a Philadelphia Congressman, suggesting that this committee in its report on the message should negative the President's assertion, and promised to supply the committee with all the information necessary for the purpose.[34]   Not content with this, he wrote to Daniel Webster, his attorney, friend and ally in the Senate, "I wish you could give a gentle impulse to the Committee of Ways & Means."[35]   Furthermore, in reply to Senator Smith's request for information as to the currency, Biddle not only supplied it but drafted and sent an outline for the Senate committee's report on the subject.[36]   The president of the Bank here embarked on a policy which would irretrievably prevent friendly relations between the President and the institution, even had Jackson had nothing else against it, and which set at naught all Biddle's disclaimers that the Bank did not and must not dabble in politics.   On March 29, and April 13, 1830, the Senate Finance and House Ways and Means Committees rendered their respective reports to Congress.   As to the national currency, Senator Smith's committee reported it to be thoroughly and entirely sound and appended some replies of Biddle's to questions on the subject of the Bank's operations and services.[37]   McDuffie's committee, reporting specifically on the part of Jackson's message relative to the Bank, stated that it was constitutional, was necessary to the point of being indispensable, had " furnished a currency more uniform than specie " and ended by pronouncing the substitute suggested by the President wholly undesirable.[38]

The Bank's friends were overjoyed.   Biddle had thousands of copies of these two reports printed both in newspapers and in pamphlet form.   These he sent to his branches

[34] Biddle to Joseph Hemphill, December 13, 14, 18, 1829, Letter Book.
[35] Biddle to Webster, February 3, 1830, Letter Book.
[36] Biddle to Sam Smith, January 18, 25, 1830, Letter Book.
[37] Niles' Register, vol. xxxviii, pp. 126–128.
[38] Ibid., pp. 183–196.

all over the country with instructions to circulate them widely.[39] He also paid John Norvall, a Philadelphia hack writer, publisher and politician, $200 for an article analyzing McDuffie's report.[40] His object in thus circulating propaganda was " so that it will be read as widely as the President's message of which it is a natural . . . antidote." [41] Had he known that Jackson was provoked at the reports, especially McDuffie's, believed the Bank responsible for influencing Congress to produce them and regarded the institution therefore as a " hydra of corruption so dangerous to our liberties," [42] Biddle might have been more cautious.

Having scattered this propaganda far and wide,[43] Biddle became very properly uneasy as to how Jackson might take it. He was not at all reassured by a rumor which reached him to the effect that Jackson had said that he would veto a bill for recharter should Congress pass one. He voiced this uneasiness to Lewis but the latter assured him that it was unfounded.[44]

This rumor was not his only ground for uneasiness. He had been warned of Van Buren's hostility to the Bank by Alexander Hamilton,[45] whose brother James was deep in the counsels of Van Buren and Jackson, and had written the part of the latter's message aimed against the Bank.[46] Biddle knew from the newspapers that Van Buren had spent a few days in Richmond, Virginia, purpose unknown.[47] About the 21st of June, 1830, Biddle received a letter from Henry Clay written in reply to one from Biddle. Speaking

---

[39] Biddle to Samuel Frothingham, May 27, 1830; to James White, May 31, 1830; to Sam Smith, April 5, 8, June 26, 1830; to McDuffie, April 19, May 10, 1830, Letter Book.
[40] Biddle to John Norvall, June 15, 1830, Letter Book.
[41] Biddle to Sam Smith, April 5, 8, 1830, Letter Book.
[42] Hamilton, Reminiscences, pp. 164, 167.
[43] Biddle to Sam Smith, April 22, 1830; to Lewis, May 8, 1830; to Edward Livingston, May 27, 1830, Letter Book.
[44] Lewis to Biddle, May 25, 1830, Biddle MSS.
[45] Hamilton to Biddle, December 10, 1829, Biddle MSS.
[46] Hamilton, Reminiscences, pp. 149, 150.
[47] Niles' Register, vol. xxxvii, pp. 172–173, 177.

of the effect of the widespread publication of the congressional reports relative to the Bank, Clay said that though they might do much to avert "the attack meditated on the B. of the U. S., you must not indulge the belief that it will escape assault. Unless I am deceived, by information, received from one of the most intelligent citizens of Virginia,[48] the plan was laid at Richmond during a recent visit made to that place by the Sec'y of State last autumn, to make the destruction of the Bank the basis of the next Presidential election. The message of the President, and other indications, are the supposed consequences of that plan."[49] How correct Clay was cannot be definitely determined. Van Buren had been in Richmond at the time named; his political relations with the Junto were close; Virginia, leader of the strict construction States, was unfavorable to the Bank; before the date of Van Buren's visit Jackson was certainly hostile to the institution and at that time was doubtless drafting his message relative to it. These circumstances taken collectively indicate a strong degree of probability that Clay was correct in his information and surmise.

Biddle now tried another means of sounding and conciliating the President. Knowing the latter's impending visit to the Hermitage,[50] on June 22 he wrote to Josiah Nicholl, cashier of his branch at Nashville, to take advantage of the President's visit to remove his errors and honest doubts regarding the Bank and if possible to discover his attitude toward recharter.[51] Nicholl was well known to Jackson and did his best. He tendered the latter apartments at his Nashville home in which the President stayed for two days. During this time Nicholl "did not neglect the subject of your letter—I enforced every argument that I could make

---

[48] Most probably Judge Francis Brooke; cf. Clay to Brooke, May 23, 1830, Clay, Correspondence, pp. 270-271.
[49] Clay to Biddle, June 14, 1830, Biddle MSS.
[50] Niles' Register, vol. xxxviii, pp. 290, 327.
[51] Biddle to Josiah Nicholl, June 22, 1830, Letter Book.

bear on the subject—or that could be of any service in re-
moving his prejudice. . . . I have taken considerable pains
and gave him all the information I consistently could on
Banking subjects. . . . I am well convinced that he will not
interfere with Congress on the subject of renewing the
Charter of the Bank." He added, however, that the President was not very communicative on the subject.[52]

Nicholl mistook Jackson completely. Less than a week
after leaving Nicholl's house Jackson wrote to a supporter
in Ohio relative to the Bank "that it should be merely a
national Bank of deposit . . . this is all the kind of a bank
that a republic should have—But if to be made a bank of
Discount as well as of deposit—I would frame its charter
upon the checks of our govt & attach it to, & make a part
of the revenue, & expose its situation as part annually to
the nation, the profits of which would then accrue to the
whole people, instead of a *few monied capitalists,* who are
trading upon our revenue, & enjoy the benefits of it, to the
exclusion of the many." [53]

Nicholl's letter reassured Biddle as to Jackson's attitude
to such an extent that he began to consider applying for
recharter at the coming session of Congress.[54] Before he
could make a move, however, a long well reasoned letter
from Clay gave him pause. Clay reaffirmed positively his
belief " That a strong party, headed by Mr. Van Buren,
some Virginia politicians, and the Richmond Enquirer, intend . . . to make the Bank question the basis of the next
presidential election," that applying for recharter at the approaching session of Congress would play into their hands
since they would merely postpone the application until the
long session, 1831–1832, and so make certain of it as a campaign issue. Clay further gave it as his opinion that the
Bank should defer application until immediately following
the presidential election.[55]

[52] Nicholl to Biddle, July 20, 1830, Biddle MSS.
[53] Jackson to Moses Dawson, July 17, 1830, Jackson MSS.
[54] Biddle to Gallatin, September 9, 1830, Letter Book.
[55] Clay to Biddle, September 11, 1830, Biddle MSS.

What Clay's underlying motive was for volunteering this advice, especially as contrasted with his later course, is not clear. It may have been disinterested friendship for Biddle and the Bank; it may have been that he hoped to defeat Jackson in 1832—his campaign having been recently launched—and so acquire the credit for himself of rechartering the Bank. Though Biddle was skeptical as to the purpose of Van Buren's Richmond trip in the previous November, Clay's letter seems to have convinced him, for he wrote the latter some six weeks later concurring in his reasoning as to the inadvisability of making a move for recharter at that time.[56]

Continuing his course of innocently offending Jackson, Biddle had just finished a bargain with Albert Gallatin whereby the latter was to write an article on banks and currency for which Biddle was to supply the needed information and to pay $1,000 for the Bank's right to publish,[57] when he was rudely awakened from his belief in Jackson's changed views by the President's second annual message. Calmly ignoring the opinion of Congress as voiced through Smith's and McDuffie's reports, Jackson again called attention to the question of rechartering the Bank, stated that nothing had occurred to lessen the dangers apprehended from it, briefly outlined his preferred substitute—a strictly national bank, to be a branch of the Treasury—and alleged, as an appeal to the States, that increased financial strength would accrue to their local banks as the result of such a measure.[58]

Biddle was awake at last to Jackson's hostility. "We shall have a great struggle with our worthy President," he wrote Gallatin, "& altho' I have no fear of the result, it

---

[56] Biddle to Clay, November 3, 1830; cf. Biddle to Robert Hunter, November 3, 1830, Letter Book.
[57] Biddle to Gallatin, June 26, December 6; to James Robertson, November 20, 1830, Letter Book.
[58] Richardson, Messages and Papers, vol. ii, pp. 528–529.

will require great caution and vigilance." [59]   " The President has now sounded the tocsin of alarm to the State Legislatures.   The Bank at this moment is in their hands—for if they choose to issue instructions they will force the members of Congress to vote against the Bank." He added that he intended to send literature favorable to the Bank " to every member of every State Legislature." [60]   Nor did the energetic Bank president expect to stop there.   To his Boston publisher he wrote: " It is . . . obvious that we shall have to make an appeal to the reason of the Country from the passions of its party leaders.   Be it so.   I have too much confidence in the sense of my Countrymen to doubt for a moment the result of that struggle: & our chief difficulty will be to place within reach of every citizen the materials of furnishing his own opinion.   This shall be done." [61]

Here is plainly set forth Biddle's plan of campaign in the struggle for recharter; namely, by the widespread circulation of propaganda to induce the state legislatures and the voters back of them to support the Bank.   It was a plan which displayed Biddle's utter ignorance of his countrymen outside of the cultured Federalist-National Republican part of the East in which he himself moved.   He had already made two serious mistakes, the first in his letter to Ingham which stirred Jackson's latent hostility, the second in scattering far and wide Smith's and McDuffie's reports.   He now decided upon the fatal one of contesting before the country the issue of recharter, and with Andrew Jackson of all men.   This last mistake was based on two fundamental misconceptions—a total failure to comprehend Jackson's strength with the masses, and the assumption that these masses formed their opinions on public questions through intelligent reading and reflection.

It was soon made evident to Biddle that the fight with the administration would be vigorously prosecuted by its sup-

[59] Biddle to Gallatin, December 28, 1830, Letter Book.
[60] Ibid., January 1, 1831.
[61] Biddle to P. P. F. Degrand, December 22, 1830, Letter Book.

porters. Almost simultaneously with Jackson's message came an attack on the Bank in the Governor of Alabama's message to his legislature.[62] From a friend in Congress came the information that Jackson had said relative to the Bank "he would be d—d if he did not pull its damned neck off yet."[63] In Congress a move to refer that part of the message relative to the Bank to a specially appointed committee instead of to the friendly Ways and Means Committee was defeated by the Bank's friends by forty-three votes.[64] Early in February, 1831, Benton delivered in the Senate a long speech against the Bank and then asked leave to introduce a resolution against it, but was refused, 23 votes to 21.[65] The newly established Globe and other Jacksonian papers thundered against the Bank in chorus.

It was at this juncture that the Bank question began really to be identified with the National Republican party.[66] This was fundamentally due to several causes. First, the superior culture, education and wealth of a large percentage of the National Republican leaders made them especially amenable to the Bank's propaganda. The second cause was the composition of the National Republican party itself. Made up of former Federalists and of the most nationalistic wing of the old Republican party it could naturally see nothing but good in an efficient, highly centralized institution such as the Bank. The third cause was the personal friendship of most of the National Republican leaders for Biddle and his institution. Prominent among these was a group of Philadelphians — John Binns, John Sergeant, Thomas Cadwalader, Horace Binney, Charles Jared Ingersoll, Robert Walsh and John Norvall—most of whom were connected with the Bank in a legal or literary capacity. In addition to these John Quincy Adams, Henry Clay, Daniel

---

[62] R. L. Colt to Biddle, December 16, 1830, Biddle MSS.
[63] Crowninshield to Biddle, December 17, 1830, Biddle MSS.
[64] Debates in Congress, 21st Cong., 2nd sess., p. 350 ff.
[65] Henry Toland to Biddle, February 2, 1831, Biddle MSS.
[66] Cf. Hammond, vol. ii, p. 350.

Webster, James Barbour, Richard Rush, Samuel Southard and Peter B. Porter, all national leaders of the party, regarded the Bank with unmixed approval and saw in it nothing but a good influence.

Other circumstances, however, were more immediately operative in identifying the Bank with the National Republican cause. The party leaders were on the alert for a better pivotal campaign issue than the unpromising subject of internal improvements, and to them the Bank looked most promising. At this time—February, 1831—the Jackson-Calhoun controversy was ready to be sprung upon the public. Calhoun had formerly been as nationalistic as Clay himself and was still supposed to be friendly to the Bank. Hence National Republican leaders hoped for a secession of Calhounites to their party,[67] and perhaps for a schism in the Democratic party which would result in a large fraction of it joining them in the effort to defeat Jackson.[68] Furthermore, Biddle's propaganda had already placed the Bank before the country and Jackson's second message had appealed to the States to take sides. The action of the Governor of Alabama was one of the effects. During the first three months of 1831, National Republican local conventions and caucuses were nominating Clay and recommending a party nominating convention. This was particularly true of Massachusetts, Maine and Connecticut, in which the Bank was specifically endorsed and named with the " American System " as part of the party program.[69]

Thus, despite his disclaimers and although he seems to have been oblivious to the fact, Biddle's Bank was already much involved in party politics. He now proceeded to involve it still more. Working through Charles J. Ingersoll, then a member of the Pennsylvania legislature, and supple-

[67] Colt to Biddle, January 29, 1831; John Sergeant to Biddle, February 19, 1831, Biddle MSS.
[68] Sergeant to Biddle, February 16, 1831, Biddle MSS.
[69] Degrand to Biddle, February 18, 24, March 5, 1831, Biddle MSS.

menting him with John Norvall,[70] he began a vigorous effort to get resolutions passed by that body declaring in favor of the Bank.   His object was to counteract a similar but hostile move from the New York legislature and thus to put the administration in fear of losing Pennsylvania.[71] His two lieutenants, with considerable indirect aid from him, succeeded in getting the desired resolution passed by a vote of 75 to 11, about the end of March.[72]   Meanwhile the Regency had introduced into the New York legislature a resolution putting that body on record as opposed to rechartering the Bank, and, in spite of a vigorous lobby engineered by Biddle through Silas Burrows,[73] passed it early in April by a strict party vote.[74]

The battle thus joined, Biddle became more energetic than ever.   He urged Webster to reply [75] to Benton's speech above mentioned, and when this was not done he himself prepared a reply " to be circulated widely throughout the United States." [76]   His principal organs of publicity were the National [Philadelphia] Gazette, the New York American, the National Intelligencer, and Duff Green's Telegraph.   In order to reach the Pennsylvania electorate more effectively, he made efforts to secure lists of individuals in the State in order to send them favorable information.[77]

All this propaganda was paid for by the Bank.   An expense book among Biddle's papers shows that the president was first authorized verbally by the directors at a meeting in 1830 to print and circulate widely Smith's and McDuffie's reports and Gallatin's article.   This expending power Biddle found to be insufficient and at another directors' meeting,

[70] Norvall to Biddle, March 2, 3, 11, 1831, Biddle MSS.

[71] Biddle to Ingersoll, February 21, 23, March 3, 1831; Ingersoll to Biddle, March 11, 1831, Biddle MSS.

[72] Ingersoll to Biddle, March 26, 1831, Biddle MSS.

[73] Silas E. Burrows to Biddle, March 7, 22, 31, April 2, 5, 7, 11, 1831, Biddle MSS.

[74] Hammond, vol. ii, pp. 350–352; G. C. Verplanck to Biddle, April 28, 1831, Biddle MSS.

[75] Biddle to Webster, January 30, 1831, Letter Book.

[76] Biddle to James Hunter, May 4, 1831, Letter Book.

[77] Biddle to Norvall, March 5, 1831, Letter Book.

March 11, 1831, "He suggested . . . the expediency . . . of extending still more widely a knowledge of the concerns of this Institution by means of the republication of other valuable articles which had issued from the daily and periodical press." He was at once given carte blanche to this end.[78] The itemized entries in this book for printing and circulating the reports of Smith and McDuffie, Gallatin's article and other literature on the Bank total, from January 1, 1830, to the end of June, 1831, $14,378.14.

The cabinet changes in 1831 put into office men much more favorable to the Bank; Edward Livingston in the State Department, Louis McLane in the Treasury and Lewis Cass in the War Department were all friends of the institution, especially the two first.[79] Woodbury of the Navy Department was non-committal, while Barry of the old cabinet and Roger B. Taney, the new Attorney-General, sided with Jackson. The entire "Kitchen Cabinet," excepting Lewis, was solidly against the Bank.[80]

Of the cabinet friends of the Bank, McLane was the most active. He conferred with Biddle in Washington and again in Philadelphia later in 1831, concerning the Bank and its prospects for recharter.[81] In the latter of these conferences, he told Biddle that in his approaching annual report as to the condition of the Treasury he expected to speak favorably of the Bank and of its recharter in preference to a new institution. He said that he had stated these intentions to the President, had explained them to him at length and that the latter had made no objection beyond a remark that he hoped the Bank issue would not be forced upon him at the ap-

---

[78] Expense book among the Biddle Papers in the Library of Congress.

[79] Hamilton to Van Buren, December 23, 1831, Van Buren MSS.; Van Buren, Autobiography, pp. 593–594.

[80] Robert M. Gibbes to Biddle, December 11, Cadwalader to Biddle, December 26, 1831, Biddle MSS.

[81] Asbury Dickins to Biddle, September 19, Wm. McIlvaine to Biddle, September 26, 1831, Biddle MSS.; memorandum in Biddle's hand dated October 19, 1831.

proaching session of Congress.[82]   McLane said further that
Livingston had been present at this conference with Jackson
and that the two Secretaries had induced the President to
say in his coming message that "having previously brought
the subject to Congress he now leaves it with them." Mc-
Lane continued that, while the President was fully confident
of his reelection, he desired it to be by a greater majority than
in 1828, and hence was loath to be forced to act on the Bank
question at all until after his election but would probably
veto it should it be forced upon him at the coming session.[83]

The news of the new cabinet's friendliness had spread
rapidly and was not without effect upon the Bank's stockholders, who held their triennial meeting on September 1,
1831.   At this meeting Biddle and the Bank directors were
especially authorized to apply for recharter of the institution
any time within the next three years that they might deem
best.[84]   In addition to this Biddle was deluged with letters
from those interested in the institution, suggesting, urging,
insisting that the coming session of Congress was the most
auspicious time for making application.[85]

True to what he had told Biddle, McLane in his report
spoke highly of the Bank's services in the past, of its indispensable utility to the government, and decidedly in favor
of the renewal of its charter with substantially no changes.[86]
At the same time Jackson's third annual message was capable
of being construed as indicative of a change in his opinions
in regard to the Bank; it was equally, however, open to the
construction that, while his own views were unchanged, he
would abide by the decision of Congress in regard to rechartering the institution.[87]   The uncertainty as to Jackson's

[82] The last session of Congress before the presidential election
in 1832.
[83] Memorandum in Biddle's hand dated October 19, 1831, Biddle
MSS.
[84] Niles' Register, vol. xli, pp. 118-119.
[85] Colt to Biddle, October 5, 7, Degrand to Biddle, October 9, J.
Cowperthwait to Biddle, November 5, 1831, Biddle MSS.
[86] Niles' Register, vol. xli, pp. 288-290.
[87] Richardson, Messages and Papers, vol. ii, p. 588.

real attitude seemed removed by McLane's report, and a rumor was speedily abroad in the East and South that the President had changed his views and would not oppose the recharter of the Bank.[88]   The message was not all that Biddle had hoped for and this, with the continued hostile tone of the administration press, still caused him uneasiness.[89] His friends and well wishers in Washington, particularly McLane and Sam Smith, assured him that all was well but that it would be dangerous to press recharter upon Jackson until after the election, as he would be likely to veto it were it thrust upon him now.[90]

What were Jackson's real views on the subject?   Professor Catterall in his " Second Bank of the United States " fell into the error of believing that Jackson at this time was favorable to the recharter of the Bank with some modifications.   Jackson's rumored change of attitude, the ambiguity in his message, and McLane's report as to the Bank caused great uneasiness among his States' Rights supporters in Virginia and South Carolina.   John Randolph of Roanoke wrote to Jackson earnestly desiring to know if the report were true, and stated that he himself had steadily refused to believe it.   To this Jackson replied:

You have done me no more than justice when you repel with indignation the charge that I had changed my views of the Bank of the United States, nothing more foreign to truth could have been said. As at present organized I have uniformly on all proper occasions held the same language in regard to that institution; and that is that it has failed to answer the ends for which it was created, and besides being unconstitutional, in which point of view, no measure of utility could ever procure my official sanction, it is on the score of mere expediency dangerous to liberty, and therefore, worthy of the denunciation which it has received from the disciples of the old republican school.

He added that McLane's report had been made on the Secretary's own authority with no intention of committing

[88] Hamilton to Van Buren, December 7, 1831, Van Buren MSS.; John Randolph to Jackson, December 19, 1831, Jackson MSS.; Niles' Register, vol. xli, p. 325.
[89] Biddle to Dickins, December 20, 1831, Letter Book.
[90] Sam Smith to Biddle, December 7, 11, 1831, Biddle MSS.

the Executive, and " in doing this he has spoken for himself and has not committed me, and I feel confident that he is the last man who would desire to commit me on such a subject." [91]

That this determination to remain uncommitted, but nevertheless hostile, on the subject of the Bank's future existence, was not a mere momentary whim but a definite policy which Jackson intended to follow—doubtless with a view to postponing the question until after the election—is shown by the following from his letter to Van Buren written the day after his message reached Congress. Enclosing to Van Buren a copy of the message and referring to the Secretary of the Treasury's report, he said, " You will find McLane differs with me on the Bank, still it is an honest difference of opinion, and in his report he acts fairly by leaving me free and uncommitted, this I will be on that subject." [92]

These passages show plainly that Jackson was consistently hostile to the Bank but preferred to remain uncommitted on the subject. His reason for this was probably twofold. In the first place he desired reelection by a larger majority than in 1828. Second, he hoped to pay off the last of the national debt by March 4, 1833, and to that end was considering the sale to the Bank of the government's 70,000 shares of stock ; hence he would naturally be loath to cause any depreciation of those shares by open hostility to the Bank at this time.[93]

Late in November, 1831, Biddle had come to no decision as to applying for recharter at the approaching session of Congress,[94] but was considering the advisability of doing so. At this time National Republican prospects were emphatically dark. Clay himself recognized the party's need for some-

---

[91] Randolph to Jackson, December 19, 1831, Jackson to Randolph, December 22, 1831, Jackson MSS.

[92] Jackson to Van Buren, December 6, 1831, Van Buren MSS.

[93] Cf. Memorandum in Biddle's hand of conversation with McLane, dated October 19, 1831, Biddle MSS.; cf. Jackson to Van Buren, November 14, McLane to Van Buren, December 14, 1831, Van Buren MSS.

[94] Biddle to Silsbee, November 21, 1831, Biddle MSS.

thing to "turn up . . . to give a brighter aspect to our affairs."[95] The party convention at Baltimore which nominated Clay, in its address to the people, clearly and definitely identified the recharter of the Bank with the party's governmental program,[96] thus carrying a step further the similar action by several state conventions earlier in the year.[97] Even after his nomination at Baltimore, Clay was far from cheerful as to the outlook.[98] With no better issue in sight than that of internal improvements at national expense, the party's position was sufficiently uncomfortable, as the removal of the Indians, the tariff and nullification were either unsuitable or unavailable.

Fully realizing this the National Republicans began efforts to secure the Bank as the much needed central issue. To have it available, it was necessary that the Bank should ask for recharter at the current session of Congress. The institution's memorial for recharter once presented, one or all of several things would work to their advantage. The question of recharter might cause a disastrous split among the Democrats,[99] since a considerable number of them in Congress and out—especially in Pennsylvania—were friendly to the Bank. Should Jackson veto a bill to that effect, it would supply the very issue which seemed to offer the best chance for defeating him. In any event such a bill's passage through Congress would enable them to act as its friends and sponsors and so identify themselves with the country's most powerful financial interests.

No sooner was Clay's election to the Senate certain,[100] than his opinion as to the advisability of the Bank deferring

---

[95] Clay to Brooke, December 9, 1831, Clay, Correspondence, p. 321.

[96] Journal of the Baltimore National Republican Convention.

[97] National Intelligencer, February 24, March 7, 1831.

[98] Clay to Brooke, December 25, 1831, Clay, Correspondence, pp. 322–323.

[99] Edward Everett to Biddle, December 14, Biddle to Gibbes, December 13, 1831, Biddle MSS.

[100] He was elected by Kentucky legislature in November, 1831, and took his seat in December.

its application for recharter until after the presidential election underwent a radical change.[101]   He wrote Biddle from Washington, December 15, asking if the latter had decided what course he would take as to application at the current session and added: " The friends of the friends of the Bank here, with whom I have conferred, seem to expect the application to be made."   He stated further that while Jackson's course in such event was uncertain, he himself believed that the President would sign a bill for recharter now, but would probably veto one after reelection.[102]   Not content with this, two days later Clay called on S. H. Smith, president of Biddle's Washington branch, and reiterated the same views more strongly, adding that should the Bank refuse to apply for recharter now, such action might be regarded by its friends among the opposition in Congress as a step unfriendly to them.[103]

Clay was by no means alone in thus urging this course upon the Bank.   Other prominent leaders of the party in and out of Congress joined in the clamor.   Prominent among these were Edward Everett, Edward Shippen of Kentucky, Charles F. Mercer of Virginia, Daniel Webster, William Creighton, Dearborn of Massachusetts, and John Williams of Tennessee.[104]

Biddle would not be committed thus hastily however. Unable to go himself, he sent his confidential agent and director, Thomas Cadwalader, to Washington about December 20, to reconnoiter the situation carefully and to ascertain upon what support in Congress the Bank could rely should it now request recharter.   Cadwalader spent some ten days at the capital and wrote Biddle his observations almost daily.

[101] John Tilford to Biddle, November 11, 1831, Biddle MSS.
[102] Clay to Biddle, December 15, 1831, Biddle MSS.
[103] S. H. Smith to Biddle, December 17, 1831, Biddle MSS.
[104] Everett to Biddle, December 5, Edward Shippen to Biddle, December 6, Mercer to Biddle, December 12, Biddle to Cadwalader, December 18, 24, Creighton to Cadwalader, December 30, Biddle to Cadwalader, December 27, 1831, Williams to Biddle, January 8, 1832, Biddle MSS.

He made a careful canvass of both Senate and House. He conferred with McLane, Sam Smith, Dallas and other well wishers of the Bank who were administration supporters, all of whom advised him that application at the current session would mean certain veto from Jackson.[105] He likewise consulted Webster and other Clay leaders and found them very eager, for party reasons, that the Bank should apply at once.[106]

Biddle placed most confidence in McDuffie,[107] Calhoun's friend, chairman of the Ways and Means Committee, and with him Cadwalader worked in closest confidence. Their joint poll of Congress indicated a majority of twenty in the House and of about three in the Senate favorable to recharter at the present session. Such being the case, wrote Cadwalader, " McDuffie leans in favor of *going it* now—and so do I." After stating that the advice of Webster and other Clay men was for immediate application, but being colored by party feeling must be discounted somewhat, he continued:

We have full confidence in McL's candour—as to his belief that Jackson will put on his veto—but the old Gent^m *may* shake in his intentions—and, if he return the Bill, he may state objections that perhaps may be yielded to by us. . . . We might be blamed [by the stockholders] for losing this session (the *long* one -moreover) & tho' we go counter to the administration men—who are interested in postponing, we keep the other party with us—some of whom w^d be lukewarm; Webster w^d be *cold*, perhaps hostile, if we bend to the Govt influence.[108]

After another conference with McLane, Sam Smith and McDuffie, at which the two former reiterated the wisdom of postponing application, Cadwalader returned to Philadelphia and reported as follows:

1. The p^t w^d be *at least* as likely to sign now, as at any future time—tho' all the information I have got leads me to the belief that he will *never* sign—2. If he is to . . . veto,—the sooner the country knows it the better—the astounding effect will have time to operate . . . a vote of 2/3d being then our only chance, the general

[105] Cadwalader to Biddle, December 21, 22, 23, 1831, Biddle MSS.
[106] Ibid., December 25, 1831, Biddle MSS.
[107] Biddle to Cadwalader, December 23, 1831, Biddle MSS.
[108] Cadwalader to Biddle, December 25, 1831, Biddle MSS.

alarm ringing through the Nation will probably secure it. . . . Mc-
Duffie, who has heard all the Secy's arguments for postponing,
agrees with me entirely in recommending an imme. application . . .
if we lose this session, he says, . . . our fate is certain—starting
now he has great hopes of eventual success by the 2/3ds if the P-
sh^d veto.[109]

Acting on this recommendation from Cadwalader as the
result of the latter's investigations, Biddle and the directors
at once drew up a memorial asking for recharter, forwarded
it to Congress January 6, 1832, where it was presented by
Dallas in the Senate January 9,[110] and by McDuffie in the
House on the same day.[111]   The Bank would have preferred
Webster as the man to present its memorial in the Senate,
but because of his party associations thought it wiser to
bring up the matter through Dallas, on account of the effect
which his being a Jackson man and from Pennsylvania
might be expected to have.[112]

In letters to Sam Smith and James Watson Webb, Biddle
stated the Bank's reasons for making present applications
for recharter as follows: (1) The unanimous wish of the
stockholders. (2) His own belief that the present was the
best time, since unless the present Congress acted upon it,
no recharter could possibly be obtained before March, 1834,
a time too near the expiration of the old charter—1836—to
permit the institution to close up its affairs satisfactorily
should its recharter be refused. He added that the Bank
took this step now, regardless of the politicians on one side
who wished to postpone it until after election, and those on
the other who wished to precipitate it.[113]

For all Biddle's disclaimers that political bias had any
weight in impelling the Bank's action, it is impossible to read

[109] Undated note in pencil, addressed to Biddle, signed " T. C.,"
and unmistakably from Cadwalader, after his return to Philadelphia.
[110] Biddle to Sam Smith, January 4, Dallas to Biddle January 9,
1832, Biddle MSS.; Biddle to Dallas, January 6, 1832, Letter Book.
[111] Biddle to McDuffie, January 6, 1832, Letter Book; Niles' Register, vol. xli, p. 363.
[112] Cadwalader to Biddle, December 26, 1831, Biddle MSS.
[113] Biddle to Sam Smith, January 4, 1832, Biddle MSS.; Biddle
to Webb, January 5, 1832, Letter Book.

Cadwalader's letters to him during the latter part of December, 1831, without being convinced that, although the pressure from Webster and other Clay leaders was not the prime factor in producing the decision for an immediate move for recharter, it certainly was not without force in contributing to that result. Thus the Bank was irretrievably committed as an election issue, and on the side of the National Republicans. Only one thing more was needed to make of it all that this party wanted—a veto by Jackson.

During the next six months Biddle employed every resource to arouse public opinion and to produce pressure upon Congress in favor of renewal. He at once wrote to every branch officer to make vigorous effort to get the citizens, and state banks if possible, in his locality to petition Congress for a recharter of the Bank of the United States.[114] He wrote to friends of the institution in all directions urging them to like exertions.[115] Unable to go in person, he sent the Bank's counsel, Horace Binney, an able lawyer, to stay in Washington and supply Dallas and McDuffie with any desired information.[116] He supplemented Binney with Charles J. Ingersoll, who remained in Washington for about two months.[117] He was persistent in his exhortations to McLane, Dallas, Binney and Ingersoll, urging, conceding, willing to agree to any modification of the charter which Jackson might desire.[118] Through the press he was incessantly active. Working through Webb's Courier and Enquirer, Gales and Seaton's National Intelligencer, Walsh's National Gazette and Duff Green's Telegraph—to all of whom the Bank made large loans during 1831 and 1832[119]—

[114] The letters in Biddle's Letter Book, latter half of January, 1832.

[115] Biddle to William B. Astor, January 16, to Robt. Oliver, January 16, to John Sergeant, January 18, 1832, Letter Book.

[116] Binney to Biddle, January 20, 23, 1832, Biddle MSS.; Biddle to Dallas, February 18, 1832, Letter Book.

[117] Ingersoll to Biddle, January 26, 1832, Biddle MSS.; Biddle to Ingersoll, March 4, 1832, Letter Book.

[118] Biddle to Binney, February 6, 13, to Ingersoll, February 6, 13, 1832, Letter Book.

[119] 22nd Cong., 1st sess., H. Rept. No. 460, pp. 86, 87, 108-110.

he had thousands of extra copies of these papers and of pamphlets containing congressional speeches in favor of the Bank printed and distributed. Near the end of March he made a hasty trip to Washington himself [120] and in May he went again and remained for some weeks.[121] Excluding the thousands of dollars in loans to friendly newspapers, on supposed good security, his direct expenditures for propaganda were comparatively light during this period, amounting, so far as can be definitely ascertained, to about $2,150 for the first six months of the year.[121]

In all these efforts for recharter Biddle was honestly working solely for his institution and without any desire to advance the cause of the National Republicans thereby. Indeed, could he have obtained Jackson's assent by making almost any concession to the President's opinion in the bill rechartering the Bank, he would gladly have done so regardless of the effect upon Clay's chances for election. That this was truly the case is shown by his letters of February 6, 11, and 13 to Ingersoll. In the first of these he urged Dallas and Ingersoll, armed with some recent resolutions of the Pennsylvania legislature in favor of the Bank, to induce the President to adopt the Bank bill, then pending in Congress, as his own measure on the ground that it appeared to be the will of the people, and thus obtain the credit for rechartering it.[122] In the letters of the 11th and 13th he wrote to the same effect, disclaimed all interest in politics, asserted that his main object was to preserve the Bank,[123] that all other considerations were insignificant and that he cared "nothing about the election."[124]

It was speedily made apparent to Biddle that he would have no easy time getting his bill through Congress. As soon as McDuffie brought up the Bank's memorial in the

---

[120] Biddle to McDuffie, April 3, 1832, Letter Book.
[121] Biddle to Webster, May 5, to Cadwalader, June 9, 1832, Biddle MSS.
[122] Biddle to Ingersoll, February 6, 1832, Letter Book.
[123] Ibid., February 11, 1832, Biddle MSS.
[124] Ibid., February 13, 1832, Letter Book.

House, Wayne of Georgia attempted to identify it with the recent National Republican convention in Baltimore, stated that it was purely a party measure, presented as it was four years before the old charter expired.[125] Cambreleng then moved that the memorial be referred to a select committee— instead of to the friendly Ways and Means Committee [126]— which would be appointed by the Speaker and therefore contain a hostile majority. Such a move would be fraught with danger for the Bank, since a long muck-raking investigation would follow with probable indefinite postponement of action. This the Bank's friends succeeded in defeating by a vote of 100 to 90, thus leaving the measure with the Ways and Means Committee.[127]

Some resolutions in the Pennsylvania legislature requesting the State's congressional delegation to work for recharter of the Bank, which passed almost unanimously about the first of February,[128] warned the Jacksonians that they must proceed warily in fighting the bill for recharter. At this time Horn, one of that State's congressmen, tried to ascertain from Jackson his sentiments as to the Bank, but "got no other satisfaction than a general answer from General Jackson that he had already said enough about it." [129] As a counter move to the Pennsylvania resolutions, the Albany Regency pushed through its legislature a resolution against recharter and requested the State's congressmen to oppose it.[130]

Ever since December, 1831, the National Republican leaders had been of the opinion that Jackson, as Clay put it, was "playing a deep game to avoid, at this session, the respon-

[125] Niles' Register, vol. xli, p. 363.
[126] Binney to Biddle, January 26, 1832, Biddle MSS.
[127] John Connell to Biddle, January 10, N. B. Van Zandt to Biddle, January 9, 11, 1832, Biddle MSS.; Niles' Register, vol. xli, pp. 363–366.
[128] John B. Wallace to Biddle, February 3, 1832, Biddle MSS.; Niles' Register, vol. xli, p. 436.
[129] Ingersoll to Biddle, February 7, 1832, Biddle MSS.
[130] Hammond, vol. ii, pp. 406–407; Niles' Register, vol. xlii, p. 77.

sibility of any decision on the Bank question." [131]   In view
of the rumors then afloat, the anxiety for postponement on
the part of McLane, Smith and other administration friends
of the Bank, and Jackson's evasiveness to Horn, there may
have been some foundation for the belief. Jackson, however, knew well the will of his party at large as to the Bank,
and with him that will was apt to be conclusive. The views
of John Randolph and James Hamilton, Jr., of South Carolina, have already been noted, as have those of Judge Catron
of Tennessee. Two other expressions of opinion reached
Jackson at about the same time as did theirs. The first,
from Willie Blount of Tennessee, with special reference to
the Bank of the United States, stated: " My notion of all
banks is, away with their Charters, that sources for corruption and aristocracy may be lessened." [132]   This represented
the average view of the somewhat uncultured and unin-
formed western Democrat. The second letter, from the son
of Alexander Hamilton, declared: " I am particularly opposed to the renewal of the present Bank for considerations
arising out of its course & not least because in making application at this time it has determined to brave the General
which it will hereafter do, at any time with success if it
should be renewed. Give this institution a Charter for 20
years longer and it is a perpetuity too strong for the government." [133]   This represents accurately the ground of opposition to the Bank of Jackson's better informed eastern
followers ; namely, that the institution was inexpedient and
dangerous to liberty. The views of Randolph, referred to
above, may be taken as typical of the southern opposition on
constitutional grounds.

Seeing that the Bank meant to force a recharter bill
through and that McDuffie meant to keep it under his wing,

---

[131] Clay to Brooke, December 25, 1831, Clay Correspondence, p.
322.
[132] Willie Blount to Jackson, November 1, 1831, Jackson MSS.
[133] James A. Hamilton to Jackson, January 12, 1832, Jackson
MSS.

the Jackson leaders in the House, working under Benton's direction, secured early in March the appointment of a special committee to inquire into the Bank's affairs and management.[134] This, being appointed by the administration Speaker, contained a majority hostile to the Bank.[135] The resulting majority report was excellently adapted to party purposes; it found the Bank guilty of subsidizing the press by loans, and of other abuses of its position. The minority report was nearly the exact opposite of that of the majority,[136] and both were made primarily for effect outside of Congress.

The result of the majority report was to make a presidential veto certain, as Biddle and the Bank's friends realized.[137] Apparently fearing the effect of so doing, Biddle would not withdraw the request for recharter and quite naturally the National Republicans would not favor the step. Accordingly, backed by the efforts of Biddle in person outside of Congress, and by those of Webster and McDuffie inside that body, the bill for recharter finally passed the House by a vote of 107 to 85,[138] and the Senate by a vote of 28 to 20.[139] This occurred during the first days of July, 1832.

The passage of the bill found Jackson's resolution unchanged. Two weeks before it occurred he wrote to Van Buren that except Taney, Woodbury and Barry, all the heads of the departments were for the Bank and added: " The coalition [meaning the National Republicans aided by Calhoun's friends] are determined to press the bank & a few more internal improvement bills on me at this session. I am prepared to meet them as I ought—but I want your aid." [140]

[134] Benton, Thirty Years' View, vol. i, pp. 235–238.
[135] Ingersoll to Biddle, March 1, Dallas to Biddle, March 15, 1832, Biddle MSS.
[136] 22nd Cong., 1st sess., H. Rept. No. 460.
[137] Biddle to Cadwalader, May 30, 1832, Biddle MSS.
[138] Niles' Register, vol. xlii, p. 352.
[139] Congressional Debates, 22nd Cong., 1st sess., vol. iii, pt. i, p. 1073.
[140] Jackson to Van Buren, June 14, 1832, Van Buren MSS.

This letter met Van Buren on his arrival in New York early in July. He at once hastened to Washington, arriving there Saturday night, July 8.[141]   He tells us:

> On the night of my . . . appearance at the White House, after my return from England, [Jackson was] stretched upon a sick bed a specter in physical appearance. . . . Holding my hand in one of his own, and passing the other through his long white locks he said, with the clearest indications of a mind composed, and in a tone entirely devoid of passion or bluster—'the bank, Mr. Van Buren is trying to kill me, *but I will kill it.'* . . . If a wish to propitiate the bank or to avoid its hostility had ever been entertained by him he might have gratified it at any moment after his accession to office.[142]

Jackson returned the bill to Congress with his veto July 10, and the effort to secure a two-thirds vote failed in the Senate, the vote being 22 to 19.[143]   The issue was fairly joined.   The National Republicans had their much needed leading issue for the campaign, and the Bank's only hope lay in joining them in defeating Jackson at the polls, either in his person direct, or by securing two-thirds of the new Congress favorable to recharter.   As Sam Smith put it in a letter to Jackson, after having urged the President to sign the bill if he could possibly see his way clear to doing so, " The mooting of the question at the present session was against my opinion.   It will however have the effect to cause all the Election to be contested on the principle of Bank or no Bank." [144]

---

[141] Creighton to Biddle, July 10, 1832, Biddle MSS.
[142] Van Buren, Autobiography, p. 625.
[143] Creighton to Biddle, July 10, 1832, Biddle MSS.; Niles' Register, vol. xlii, pp. 365–368, 378–379.
[144] Sam Smith to Jackson, June 17, 1832, Jackson MSS.

CHAPTER VI

THE CONCLUSION OF THE CAMPAIGN

The presidential campaign of 1832 differed essentially from the two immediately preceding it. The former had been contests between factions of the old Republican party, their issues had been confined chiefly to the personalities of the candidates, and the voter had been distinctively known as an Adams, a Jackson, a Clay or a Calhoun man, according to the leader of his faction. The campaign of 1832 was between three definitely organized political parties, each with a more or less definite governmental program in view, and each emphasizing that policy before the personality of its candidate. In 1824, and for the most part in 1828 also, campaign issues had been utilized principally for their effect in electing the particular candidate supported, rather than for themselves as issues; in 1832 the nominees were entered by their respective parties as champions of particular principles, these principles taking precedence over the candidates in relative importance.

With the single exception of nullification, Jackson himself supplied all the issues on which his campaign for reelection was fought and upon which his newly established Democratic party rested. In its larger aspects, therefore, the campaign was a decisive test before the country of his work and of his party's stability as a political organization. The principles which were now the campaign issues had, for the most part, been evolved with the party during Jackson's first administration.

When elected in 1828, Jackson cannot be said to have been the leader of a political party; his following was too heterogeneous for that. At that time, excluding a few Federalists and the followers of Adams and Clay, Jackson's support embraced all of the old Republican party as it had been in Monroe's day. This strength was clearly reflected in the vote for Speaker of the Congress elected with Jackson, when Stevenson received 152 votes against 39 for all others.[1] This large following was not destined to remain intact and to become in toto the new Democratic party. Such might have been the result had Jackson carried on the old Monroe policies with their leanings toward nationalism.

The successive development and application of Jackson's policy and constitutional views as to removals from office, the Indian question, internal improvements, the choice of a successor, nullification, and the Bank, made it impossible to keep together the following which had elected him in 1828. Each of these issues in turn caused the defection of a relatively small number of supporters. The large majority which steadfastly supported him through these various secessions, or elimination processes, was the new Democratic party properly speaking. All of these questions collectively were the issues of the campaign, but the most important and the one which was the final test of Jackson's political judgment and leadership, and the principal issue on which the contest turned, was the Bank. How the latter came to occupy the foremost place has already been described.

After noticing very briefly the effect of the above-mentioned issues in reducing Jackson's original following, it will be in order to notice the conduct of the Bank and its effect on the campaign during the contest's concluding months.

The chief article in Jackson's political creed was what Benton called[2] the *demos krateo* principle—the commons to govern—and he possessed an intuitive ability to interpret that body's will. Jackson himself expressed it thus: "you know, I never despair. I have confidence in the virtue & good sense of the people."[3] Herein lay his strength during

---

[1] Niles' Register, vol. xxxvii, p. 254.
[2] Benton, vol. i, p. 46.
[3] Jackson to Van Buren, November 1, 1830, Van Buren MSS.

his presidency, both as executive and as party leader.[4] It was in obedience to his honest interpretation of the people's will that he reversed his views in 1824 [5] and inaugurated the removal from office of those whom he believed to be the political tools which a corrupt administration had used to defeat the popular will.[6] In appointing his friends to these offices, Jackson merely did what both Clay and Edward Everett had strongly advocated during Adams' administration.[7] The removals and appointments, beyond alarming Calhoun [8] and alienating a few men like John McLean,[9] had little effect on Jackson's following save to strengthen its confidence in its leader.   Aside from introducing a bad precedent, the effect of the removals was beneficial in that it strengthened the President's control of the executive departments, thereby promoting the independence of the executive branch of the government.

Jackson's decision to remove the Indians to reservations west of the Mississippi, or else to leave them entirely in the hands of Georgia, Alabama and Mississippi,[10] caused the defection of many pious people like the Quakers, whose kindness of heart and missionary zeal far outran their knowledge of the actual state of affairs.[11] The opposition seized upon this question as the first ground for attacking the administration, a preliminary test of strength, a " feeling out " of the country.[12] Such losses as Jackson sustained from it were confined to the East and, it is reasonable to believe, were

---

[4] Van Buren, Autobiography, pp. 226, 253, 449, 543.

[5] Jackson to Donelson, April 11, 1824, Donelson MSS.

[6] Jackson to Van Buren, March 31, 1829, Jackson MSS.

[7] Clay to Webster, April 14, 1827, Webster MSS.; Everett to McLean, August 1, 18, 1828, McLean MSS.

[8] Calhoun to McLean, September 22, 1829, McLean MSS.

[9] Joseph E. Sprague to McLean, March 23, 1829, William Slade to McLean, March 23, 1829, McLean MSS.; Cambreleng to Van Buren, April 28, 1829, Van Buren MSS.

[10] Jackson to Ingham, July 31, 1830, John Coffee to Jackson, September 29, 1830, Jackson MSS.

[11] Van Buren, Autobiography, pp. 284-285; 288-289.

[12] Ibid., pp. 287-289.

largely balanced by the effect on the West and Southwest, where removal of the Indians was highly popular.

The Maysville veto, with the decisive check it administered to the general inclination for internal improvements at national expense, caused the first notable, and perhaps the largest, secession from the Jackson ranks. The bill in question had passed the House by a vote of 96 to 87 [13] before the President's attitude was definitely known,[14] and the attempt to pass it over his veto had 97 votes for, to 90 opposed. This indicates a distinct falling off in the strength which elected Stevenson administration speaker six months earlier. It marked the first sharp drawing of party lines on the basis of principle. This is not surprising since the veto was in effect a direct blow at one wing of the National Republican basic doctrine, the "American System." The National Republicans, eager to gather into their fold the fragments broken away from the Jackson party by the veto, as heretofore noted, launched their campaign for Clay as soon as the presidential negative of the Maysville Road Bill had had time to circulate through the country.

Almost exactly coincident with the Maysville veto came Jackson's break with Calhoun, the outcome of the contest for the succession between the latter and Van Buren. Only six weeks before the break the President's attitude against nullification had been made known. These two factors operated to counteract each other to some extent in their effect on the party. Jackson's course toward Calhoun and his partiality for Van Buren operated unfavorably for the President's party among Calhoun's admirers both North and South. It was this which quickened the hopes of the National Republicans just prior to launching Clay's campaign.[15] On the other hand, Jackson's resolute "Our Federal Union —it must be preserved," together with Calhoun's open advo-

---

[13] Niles' Register, vol. xxxviii, p. 183.
[14] Van Buren, Autobiography, pp. 322–325.
[15] Clay to Brooke, April 24, 1830, Webster to Clay, May 29, 1830, Clay, Correspondence, pp. 262–265, 275–276.

cacy of nullification, strengthened the Executive in both East and North.[16]

The part of Jackson's original following, whose loyalty to him thus far had remained unshaken, underwent another reduction in consequence of his attack on the Bank. The losses, however, which his party sustained in the course of that encounter, down to the end of 1832, were less than those entailed by his veto of the Maysville Road Bill. This was due in part to the fact that in proportion as his following had been diminished by the issues just referred to, the residue was proportionately unlikely to be affected; partly to the innate hostility of the masses, the bulk of his party, to wealth in general; and partly to the fact that the Bank did not become a campaign issue, in the full sense, until Jackson's veto of the recharter bill in July, 1832.

The campaign entered its last stage with the May conventions of 1832, of which the Democratic has already been described. The National Republican convention of young men which met in Washington May 7 to 12,[17] pursuant to call by the convention of the party at Baltimore,[18] was in all respects an electioneering move designed to stir party enthusiasm. Ostensibly, its primary object was the ratification of Clay's nomination and this it proceeded to do on the third day of its session.[19] Immediately following this began the real work for which the young men had been assembled,— the adoption of measures for setting forth the party's platform and for appealing to the country. For these objects two committees, each containing a member from each State present, were appointed. The duty of one of these commit-

---

[16] Van Buren, Autobiography, pp. 415–417; Hamilton to Jackson, September 1, 1831, Jackson MSS.

[17] National Intelligencer, May 8–14, 1832.

[18] Convention of National Republican Party at Baltimore, December, 1831, Niles' Register, vol. xli, p. 305; Journal of the National Republican Convention.

[19] Proceedings of the National Republican Convention of Young Men . . . Washington, May 7, 1832, in Historical Pamphlets, vol. 293, No. 18, Johns Hopkins University Library.

tees was to draft the usual address, that of the other to draw up " resolutions upon such subjects as shall be deemed proper to be acted upon by this Convention." [20]

The first of these documents, the address " to the Young Men of the United States," was similar in all respects to the usual party appeal of this kind, although it should be understood that the manifestos issued by the party conventions of the period differed essentially from the present-day platform, first in being solely a justification of, or sort of apologia for, the action of the bodies from which they issued ; second in dwelling almost entirely upon the errors and evils of the opponent's policy, with little or nothing said, save by implication, as to their own constructive program. The first party platform in the modern sense was the second document drawn up by the convention, " the Resolutions." [21] The first four of these resolutions stated clearly the party's advocacy of a protective tariff, internal improvements at national expense, and the maintenance of the Supreme Court's authority and jurisdiction. The remainder were of a denunciatory character, severely criticizing the removals from office as violations of the spirit and letter of the Constitution, the administration's course as to the New England boundary dispute, and the West Indian trade controversy. The resolutions closed with the present-day declaration that the safety, honor and welfare of the union demanded the election of the National Republican candidates. [22]

This convention, barring the platform, produced no innovations in convention practice that had not already been applied by one or another of the similar party convocations. Its proceedings included an invitation to Clay to be present in person to deliver a short speech and to meet the delegates, some 315 in number. There was a pilgrimage of the convention in a body to Mount Vernon, and a visit by a special

---

[20] Ibid.
[21] For complete resolutions, see Appendix III.
[22] Proceedings of the National Republican Convention of Young Men.

committee to pay the party's respects to Charles Carroll of Carrollton. This latter courtesy was the way in which each of the three major party conventions expressed its veneration for the founders of the republic.

The dire need of the National Republicans for a campaign issue and their eagerness to have the Bank commit itself as such has already been mentioned. In the seven months between Clay's nomination at Baltimore and Jackson's veto of the bill rechartering the Bank, the hopes of the party for success did not rise very high. Clay's refusal to come out against the Masonic order and the Antimasonic nomination of Wirt split in two the potential vote against Jackson. If the latter was to be defeated, there was truly need for union in the opposition, both National Republican and Antimasonic. A careful observer wrote Jackson as early as July, 1831, before the Bank had committed itself to the National Republicans: "Upon a comparison of facts carefully collated for some time past from a mass of newspapers from every State in the Union, inimical and friendly, and the examination of several hundred toasts drank [on the 4th of July, 1831], . . . I set it down with the utmost confidence in the accuracy of the prediction, that, if *your* life is spared, *you* will be again sworn in as President . . . on the 4th of March, 1833." The writer added further that he was certain of the sentiments of Maine, New Hampshire, New York, Pennsylvania, Virginia, the two Carolinas and Georgia.[23] In November, 1831, Richards, mayor of Philadelphia, wrote McLean that Jackson's election appeared certain.[24] We have noticed elsewhere Clay's own rather gloomy views expressed in December, 1831; indeed, it was reported at that time, with perhaps some basis of truth, that Clay's nomination by the National Republicans at Baltimore had been "not with any hope of his success at the next election, but for future use, and to

[23] Charles G. DeWitt to Jackson, July 20, 1831, Jackson MSS.
[24] Richards to McLean, November 11, 1831, McLean MSS.

prevent him from sinking into oblivion as a candidate for the Presidency."[25]

However this last might be, it was plainly evident early in 1832 that Jackson's popularity was not appreciably diminished,[26] and that unless a union could be effected between Antimasons and National Republicans his election was a foregone conclusion. A letter written by William Wirt, the Antimasonic candidate, to John McLean at this time is important, both as emphasizing this fact and as indicating Wirt's entire indifference to the Antimasons:

I lament with you the inefficiency of the opposition. If it were merely an opposition to the present order of things it would unite and become efficient. But the opposition itself is formed of self asserting materials. How is this intestine war among the very elements of the opposition to be overcome? The National Republicans would not leave their present nomination for any other man in the Union. Their candidate will infallibly keep the field. Neither the Anti-tariff nor the Antimasonic party will unite upon him; and his party will unite upon no other. So that the defeat of the opposition seems at present to be unavoidable. *And they all know it.* Yet not an advance is made or even meditated toward conciliation. If they would consent to set aside the whole array of nominees & agree upon a new name, the object might be accomplished. The Antimasons would do this, in favor of one individual [McLean], and they would have my most hearty concurrence. But the National Republicans will never consent to abandon their first choice to come to that individual. . . . It is easy to see what reason and patriotism dictate in the case—but the small still voice of reason and patriotism is drowned amidst the roar and din of contending factions. For my own part, I have held but one language to the Antimasons from the beginning—which is that I consider their nomination of me as their own work—that it is their perfect right to change it whenever they please, and that my opinion, it is their duty to change it, if by so doing, they can prevent the reelection of the present incumbent without any material sacrifice of their own principle and this they could do &, I am persuaded would do, if the National Republicans could be prevailed on to unite in the measure. But these last say, on the other hand, that they cannot do so without entirely sacrificing their own principles—for they consider their candidates as identified with their principles & the very existence of their party. So that the greater considerations of the *Country,* of the constitution and the union is to be sacrificed to the triumph of a party, or rather to an effort at triumph which they cannot but know must end in defeat. So that it is not the want of skill nor of perseverance . . . which is to ruin us . . .

25 Jackson to Van Buren, December 17, 1831, Van Buren MSS.
26 M. T. Simpson to McLean, February 8, 1832, McLean MSS.

it is wilful obstinacy and perseverance in a cause which they know will be fatal. Heaven have mercy on us for that alone can save us.[27]

It would seem from this distance that the union of the two parties would have been easily possible but for the National Republican obstinacy in courting certain defeat in preference to giving up Clay; for, while the Antimasons were not greatly interested as a party in the questions of internal improvements, tariff, and Bank, the fact that their strongholds were in New England, New York, Pennsylvania and Ohio presupposes among a considerable part of their voters, at least, a preference for a nationalistic policy regarding these questions. According to Thurlow Weed, the Antimasons sympathized with Clay's views, particularly on the tariff.[28] From this it is apparent that no sacrifice of National Republican principles would have been entailed by effecting at once the union with the Antimasons, which they resorted to two years later.

Wirt was not alone in the opinion that the refusal of the National Republicans to give up Clay and unite with the Antimasons in supporting some other candidate against Jackson would produce the defeat of them both.[29] This need for unity in the opposition against Jackson was clearly felt by both Antimasons and National Republicans, and even by the disgruntled followers of Calhoun. Calhoun himself, his friend and ally, Governor Floyd of Virginia, and Duff Green, as early as March, 1832, seriously considered placing the South Carolinian in the field as a presidential candidate. Accordingly they approached Clay's friends with the proposition that the latter should unite with them in supporting Calhoun in the South and Southwest, provided it should appear that, thus supported, the latter could carry several

[27] William Wirt to McLean, April 17, 1832, McLean MSS.
[28] Cf. Weed, Autobiography, p. 350; Clay to Johnston, July 23, 1831, Clay, Correspondence, p. 309.
[29] Cf. Weed, p. 391; John Norvall to McLean, January 20, John W. Taylor to McLean, May 18, B. W. Richards to McLean, June 5, 1832, McLean MSS.

states.   The object of such a scheme, aside from the motive
of revenge on Calhoun's part, was to bring the election of
president into the House of Representatives where Clay's
chances would be infinitely better.[30]   Nothing more appears
relative to the plan, and as Calhoun was not brought out for
president, and as the Clay party in Virginia chose Clay electors,[31] the presumption is that Calhoun's friends perceived
the impossibility of his carrying any State save his own and
gave up the idea.

   The opposition to Van Buren's vice-presidential candidacy
by the Calhoun faction has already been noticed, together
with its failure to prevent his nomination at the Baltimore
Convention in May, 1832.   The South Carolinian's managers
then transferred their activities again to Virginia, the Carolinas, and Alabama, their object being to nominate Barbour
with Jackson on a separate ticket,[32] as had been done by the
opposition to Van Buren within the Democratic party in
Pennsylvania.   Accordingly they held a state nominating
convention at Charlottesville, Virginia, June 12–14, nominated Jackson and Barbour, appointed a corresponding
committee, drew up the customary address and chose electors
favorable to Barbour instead of Van Buren.[33]   It was followed by another similar convention and a like result in
North Carolina, June the 18th.   To the North Carolina Convention's notification to him of his nomination, Barbour returned an appreciative but equivocal reply, neither accepting
nor declining.[34]   In South Carolina Barbour was nominated
for vice-president by a local meeting in the Laurens district,
the bulk of the State being apparently too much absorbed

[30] Clay to Brooke, April 1, 1832, Clay, Correspondence, pp. 332–
333.
   [31] Niles' Register, vol. xlii, p. 327; Stevenson to Ritchie, February 4, C. W. Gooch to Cambreleng, October 9, 1832, Van Buren
MSS.
   [32] John Randolph to Jackson, July 5, 15, 1832, Jackson MSS.
   [33] Richmond Enquirer, June 19, 1832; Niles' Register, vol. xlii,
pp. 303–304.
   [34] Ibid., pp. 339, 406.

with nullification to think much about opposing Van Buren by means of the ballot.[35] In Alabama the attempt to place Barbour on the Jackson ticket seems to have failed completely.[36]

Barbour's course in regard to this movement was peculiar but is not hard to explain. Since 1830 he had been a Judge of the United States District Court in Virginia,[37] and was in the good graces of the administration. It is not improbable that he had his eyes on a seat on the national Supreme Bench. Hence he would naturally be chary of offending the power from which his appointment must come. His nomination in opposition to Van Buren did not meet with administration approval, as the tone of the Globe soon showed.[38] In spite of this and of pressure from the Junto, Barbour was loath to withdraw his name,[39] and it was not until the very eve of the election that he decided to jeopardize his future no further, and withdrew his name from the Democratic ticket. The reason he alleged for his withdrawal was that the opposition party was using his nomination as a basis for proclaiming that a division existed in the Democratic party.[40] His action was, however, sufficiently early to placate the administration and to admit of Jackson appointing him to the Supreme Court about the end of 1835.[41]

While this had been going on in the South during the hottest of the campaign, a definite move was made toward a combination of National Republican and Antimasonic forces in New York, to enable the latter with National Republican aid to win the control of the State from the Democrats. In return for this, the National Republic .. expected the support of the Antimasonic electors to be given to Clay. It was the first step toward what became, in the North at least, a

[35] Ibid., vol. xlii, p. 405.
[36] Jackson to Van Buren, September 16, 1832, Van Buren MSS.
[37] Niles' Register, vol. xxxix, p. 121.
[38] Ibid., vol. xlii, p. 406.
[39] C. W. Gooch to Cambreleng, October 9, 1832, Van Buren MSS.
[40] Letter of withdrawal dated October 24, 1832, published in Richmond Enquirer, October 30, 1832; also in Niles' Register, vol. xliii, p. 153.
[41] Niles' Register, vol. xlix, p. 300.

complete merging of both parties in the Whigs two years later. In pursuance of this plan, the presidential electors of the Antimasonic party were unpledged to any candidate, and the subsequent National Republican state convention adopted Granger and Stevens, the Antimasonic gubernatorial ticket, together with the Antimasonic slate of presidential electors, as its own. To further the coalition and prevent discord between the two parties in making their local nominations in the districts and counties, one National Republican and one Antimason, Matthew L. Davis and Thurlow Weed, were selected by their respective parties to make the rounds of the local conventions to unite them upon the same candidates for the legislature and other state offices.[42] This junction of forces was rendered the more feasible since both parties in the State favored the Bank and the "American System." [43]

This coalition gave the Democrats of the Regency no uneasiness. The fact that neither Antimasons nor National Republicans dared avow whom their presidential electors, if chosen, would vote for, made a fine subject for ridicule for the Democratic press which referred to the coalition as the "Siamese Twin Party," on account of the peregrinations about the State of Davis and Weed.[44] The Regency convention nominated William L. Marcy as its candidate for governor,[45] and Van Buren himself took charge of the campaign. In the course of a tour through the State, he wrote to Jackson the following: " The union between the different sections of the opposition, is, on the face of it quite imposing, but you may rest assured that we shall give them a sound beating. . . . I can with truth say that the election field never presented so pleasant an aspect to me as at this time." [46]

[42] William Rupell to McLean, May 14, 1832, Albert H. Tracy to McLean, October 19, 1832, McLean MSS.; Weed, 413–414; Hammond, vol. ii, p. 417.

[43] McCarthy, The Antimasonic Party, p. 413, based on Thurlow Weed's Albany Evening Journal, August 24, September 14, 1832.

[44] Hammond, vol. ii, pp. 417–418; Weed, pp. 413–414.

[45] Hammond, vol. ii, pp. 421–423.

[46] Van Buren to Jackson, August 29, 1832, Van Buren MSS.

One of the principal grounds on which Van Buren was attacked after his nomination on the ticket with Jackson was his tariff attitude.   In the South it was feared that he did not favor reduction of the tariff, and in the North he was suspected of opposing protection.   The uneasiness in the party on this subject, even before he returned from Europe, led Jackson to write him, " They enemies have attempted to assail you on your ultra tariff opinions.   I have said you were for a fair protection to place our productive labour on a fair competition with that of Europe &c &c." [47]

Van Buren, as a matter of fact, had supported the Tariff of 1828.[48]   This record, together with the allegations of the opposition, coupled with the movement in favor of Barbour, and Jackson's action in signing a bill for some internal improvements whose national character was dubious,[49] caused considerable uneasiness among the Democratic leaders in the South.   To such an extent were they carried by their fears that Daniel and Ritchie, of the Junto, and John Forsyth of Georgia wrote Van Buren urging him to take "the first opportunity of putting yourself right on the subject of the tariff of 1828," [50] to work for a reduction of duties in order to conciliate South Carolina, and, for its effect on the party at large, to come out strongly on old Democratic principles.[51] Further point was added to these exhortations by a political meeting held at Shocco Springs, North Carolina, on August 25.   Through a committee it addressed to both Van Buren and Barbour a request to be informed of their sentiments " on the subjects of the protective system and its proper adjustment, internal improvements, the Bank of the United States and nullification." [52]

[47] Jackson to Van Buren, July 7, 1832, Van Buren MSS.
[48] Van Buren Autobiography, p. 171.
[49] Niles' Register, vol. xlii, p. 382.
[50] Forsyth to Van Buren, July 7, 1832, Van Buren MSS.
[51] Ritchie to Van Buren, July 10, P. V. Daniel to Van Buren, July 12, 1832, Van Buren MSS.
[52] Quoted by Van Buren from the Shocco Springs Committee's resolutions of enquiry. See Appendix II.

This inquiry reached Van Buren in the midst of a trip into western New York about the first of October. Coming on the heels of the Junto's uneasiness, it decided him to speak. His reply, written largely in pencil and while traveling in stage coaches and canal boats, dated October 4,[53] was published first in the Albany Argus.[54] This document constitutes the best statement anywhere to be found of the principles which Jackson had established as the party tenets.[55] Jackson wrote with reference to it: "I have seen and read with much pleasure your reply to the Committee of N. Carolina. It breathes the same principles and opinions I assured your friends you always possessed—All my pledges on this score you have redeemed. Your reply meets the approbation of all your friends and must silence your enemies."[56] This letter of Van Buren's was published by Blair in pamphlet form in 1834, presumably for party use in the next presidential campaign. In the present campaign, together with Jackson's veto message on the Bank, it formed the party's chief campaign literature of the more substantial type.

In this reply Van Buren discussed the subjects in the order inquired about. He declared his belief in the power of Congress to enact tariff legislation, but stated that he was opposed to any tariff which operated unequally on different parts of the country and added that the near extinction of the public debt made tariff reduction further desirable, quoting Jackson's third annual message on this point.[57] Concerning internal improvements he expressed the same views as those of Jackson's Maysville veto; namely, that the national government was without constitutional authority to construct directly internal improvements within a State, but

[53] Van Buren, Autobiography, p. 562.
[54] Niles' Register, vol. xliii, p. 125.
[55] Van Buren's reply, Pamphlet under this caption in Van Buren MSS.; cf. Autobiography, p. 567; see Appendix II.
[56] Jackson to Van Buren, October 23, 1832, Van Buren MSS.
[57] Cf. Richardson, Messages and Papers, vol. ii, pp. 556.

might aid financially such works of improvement as were national, as distinguished from local, in character. Concerning the Bank and nullification he stated unequivocally his belief that both were unconstitutional, and that the latter, in addition, would entail " the ultimate but certain destruction of the Confederacy."

Jackson returned the Bank Bill with his veto on July 10, 1832.[58] Coming at this time, and in view of the National Republicans' attitude toward the Bank, the veto made it certain that " Bank or no Bank "[59] would be the main issue of the campaign. Both National Republicans and Democrats were alike pleased that such was the case. " If Jacksonism," wrote Watmough to Biddle, " can stand this, it will stand anything & we may as well give up the rule to vulgarity & Barbarism at once."[60] Biddle wrote to Clay, " the President . . . must pay the penalty of his own rashness. As to the veto message, I am delighted with it. . . . It is really a manifesto of anarchy such as Marat or Robespierre might have issued to the mob of the Faubourg St. Antoine; and my hope is, that it will contribute to relieve the country from the dominion of these miserable people. You are destined to be the instrument of that deliverance."[61] On the Democrats' side, Peter V. Daniel wrote Van Buren: " I greatly rejoice at the President's rejection of the Bank Bill."[62] Van Buren said: " The Veto is popular [in New York] beyond my most sanguine expectations. I have not heard of a single case where it has driven a friend from us . . . and for the first time since I have taken part in politics, have I found a prominent measure of an opposing candidate extensively applauded by his adversaries."[63]

[58] Ibid., vol. ii, pp. 576–591.
[59] Sam Smith to Jackson, June 17, 1832, Jackson MSS.
[60] Watmough to Biddle, July 10, 1832, Biddle MSS.
[61] Biddle to Clay, August 1, 1832, Clay, Correspondence, p. 341.
[62] Daniel to Van Buren, July 12, 1832, Van Buren MSS.
[63] Van Buren to Donelson, August 26, 1832, Van Buren MSS.

The veto message, probably the joint work of Jackson and Taney,[64] was an excellent campaign document, and in that part dealing with the constitutional aspects of the case, an able, well-reasoned production. As a friend in the Senate wrote Biddle, it was written for effect and as an appeal to the country.[65] It objected to the Bank as unconstitutional, as a monopoly, as unnecessary, inexpedient and injurious to the country, and supplemented these objections by an appeal to the natural dislike of poverty for wealth, to the prejudices of the state banks and to the national prejudice against foreign stockholders.[66]

Both parties, Democrats and National Republicans—the Bank's cause being so enthusiastically pushed by the latter as to exclude practically all else—now joined battle in good earnest.[67] The Democrats had manifested their confidence in the efficacy of the veto as an aid to their cause by moving in Congress that 16,000 copies of the message should be printed for use of the members.[68] So great was the confidence of the National Republican Congressmen in its good effects upon their cause that they joined the Democrats in passing the resolution. Nor did their party's error end there. Their press, aided by the Bank, printed and circulated it by thousands, together with the speeches against it in the Senate by Clay and Webster.[69] Indeed the expense account of the Bank contains an item of $558 expended for printing, wrapping and distributing 30,000 copies of "General Jackson's veto."[70]

In addition to supplying their leading issue, the Bank was incidentally a valuable financial ally of the National Repub-

---

[64] Cf. Jackson to Van Buren, July 7, 1832, Van Buren MSS.; cf. Taney to Jackson, June 27, 1832, Jackson MSS.

[65] J. S. Johnston to Biddle, July 10, 1832, Biddle MSS.

[66] Richardson, Messages and Papers, vol. ii, pp. 576–591.

[67] Watmough to Biddle, July 13, 1832, Biddle MSS.

[68] Niles' Register, vol. xlii, pp. 361, 379.

[69] Clay to Webster, August 27, 1832, Webster MSS.; Watmough to Biddle, September 25, 1832, Biddle MSS.; Biddle to Webster, October 14, 1832, Letter Book.

[70] Expense Book in Biddle MSS.; 23rd Cong., 2nd sess., S. Doc. No. 17, p. 325.

licans. The institution's expense account shows a total of $16,999.00 applied, during the last half of 1832, to the publishing and distributing of the veto message, speeches of Clay, Webster and Ewing, and other literature favorable to the Bank. From the beginning of 1830 to the end of 1832 the Bank spent for propagandic and campaign purposes certainly above $42,000.00, a sum at least the equivalent of half a million expended in a campaign of today.[71]

The first indication bearing on the general results of the efforts of both parties was the election of state officers in Kentucky during August. Both sides relied mainly on the Bank issue and made a liberal use of the veto message. The Democrats, however, had the better organization and diffused their literature more widely.[72] On the other hand the veto of the Bank bill aided the National Republicans considerably since it caused a small financial panic in some places.[73] This contest in Clay's supposed stronghold resulted in the election of Breathitt, the Jackson candidate for governor, by a majority of some twelve hundred, although Clay's forces succeeded in electing their candidate for lieutenant-governor and a majority of the legislature.[74]

This failure of the National Republicans to carry Kentucky entirely had a depressing effect on them and correspondingly encouraged the Democrats. Clay wrote Webster in rather gloomy vein lamenting the superior industry of the Jacksonians in " the circulation of documents " and the slowness with which their own party had acted in this respect.[75] To Biddle he wrote in the same strain: " I . . . sincerely hope that the overthrow which you anticipate, of our present misguided rulers will be realized. . . . I transmit under your cover a letter . . . which . . . contains a faithful account

[71] Ibid., Expense Book in Biddle MSS.

[72] Clay to Webster, August 27, 1832, Webster MSS.

[73] John Breathitt to Jackson, August 23, 1832, Jackson MSS.; Niles' Register, vol. xlii, pp. 407, 425, 427.

[74] Niles' Register, vol. xliii, p. 3.

[75] Clay to Webster, August 27, 1832, Webster MSS.

of our recent elections. Their result was certainly not satis-
factory, in all respects." [76]   At this time Van Buren, in writing
Jackson from New York, added to his letter: " P. S.   B's
[Breathitt's election in Kentucky] is truly a glorious affair.
You can form no idea of the effect it has had upon the poor
Clay men in this quarter." [77]

Jackson himself watched the public sentiment closely.
He had a fair opportunity of observing for himself the situation in the South, the West and the Southwest as he trav-
ersed Virginia, Tennessee and Kentucky in the course of his
trip to the Hermitage from July to October.[78]   In addition,
while at the Hermitage, he received reports from friends and
party leaders in different quarters of the country.[79]   His estimate of the outlook was as follows: " The veto works well,"
he wrote Donelson, " instead of crushing me as was expected
& intended, it will crush the Bank." [80]   To Van Buren he
wrote: " Mr. Clay will not get one Electoral vote west of the
mountains or south of the Potomac, in my opinion." [81]   " I
have twice passed through Virginia at different points on my
journey to & from the Hermitage—I have no hesitation in
assuring you, that it is my opinion, that you will get the vote
of every state that I will, except S. Carolina, and it is doubt-
full whether she will give her vote to either of us." [82]

Even men who were disinterested in the election's outcome
and not unfriendly to Clay regarded the result as a foregone
conclusion from the time the Bank veto was fairly before the
country.   Richards wrote McLean: " I think the bank cannot
now be rechartered, it threw itself upon the support of the
Clay party and relied upon the fears of Jackson to secure it

[76] Clay to Biddle, August 27, 1832, Biddle MSS.
[77] Van Buren to Jackson, August 29, 1832, Van Buren MSS.
[78] Jackson to Andrew Jackson, Jr., July 19, 1832, Jackson MSS.;
Globe, October 20, 1832.
[79] Cf. Van Buren to Jackson, August 29, 31, Jackson to Van
Buren, August 30, September 16, October 23, 1832, Van Buren MSS.
[80] Jackson to Donelson, August 9, 1832, Donelson MSS.
[81] Jackson to Van Buren, September 16, 1832, Van Buren MSS.
[82] Ibid., October 23, 1832.

his signature at the last moment. It has miscalculated on both grounds. The Clay party will gain nothing on the Bank question in this State [Pennsylvania] and will lose elsewhere. Attachment to a large monied corporation is not a popular attribute. The feeling of common minds is against Mr. Clay."[83] McLean himself expressed this opinion: "I do not believe that the veto will lose the general the vote of any State; and his election, I consider, as certain as any future event can be. His opponent will fall below the last vote of Mr. Adams."[84]

The election returns fulfilled these prophecies excepting only as to Pennsylvania and Kentucky. The result was a victory for Jackson by an electoral vote unequalled, when two or more parties participated, since the days of Washington. Wirt and Ellmaker obtained only the seven votes of Vermont. Clay and Sergeant received the entire vote of Massachusetts, Rhode Island, Connecticut, Delaware and Kentucky, and five from Maryland—a total of 49. Excepting South Carolina's, Jackson received every remaining electoral vote save two not cast in Maryland,[85]—a total of 219 of the 288 in the electoral college. Van Buren did nearly as well; he received the same electoral vote as did Jackson less the 30 votes of Pennsylvania which went to Wilkins. In South Carolina and Delaware presidential electors were still appointed by the legislature. Since the nullificationists wholly controlled the former State, it is not strange that its 11 votes went to Calhoun's friend, John Floyd of Virginia.[86]

The popular vote defies exact calculation. Based on the returns given in Niles' Register, probably the most accurate source available, and supplemented by conservative estimates, based on the individual State's population, its general attitude toward the candidates and the issues, and on such figures for

---

[83] Richard to McLean, July 19, 1832; cf. ibid., October 25, 1832, McLean MSS.

[84] McLean to Robert Walsh, July 29, 1832, McLean MSS.

[85] This was due to the illness of two electors.

[86] See table, Appendix IV.

local elections as can be found, it is a safe statement that of the popular vote Jackson received about 661,000, Clay about 454,000 and Wirt about 100,000. It is therefore approximately correct to estimate Jackson's majority at 100,000,[87] though this is some 30,000 less than Stanwood's somewhat erroneous tabulation.[88]

The National Republican and Antimasonic opposition to Jackson owed its defeat primarily to the popularity with the larger part of the electorate of Jackson's measures, the latter based on his intuitive perception of the will of the masses, reinforced by his personal popularity on the one hand, and to the alliance of West and South, fortified by New York, on the other hand. Jackson's policy was sufficiently acceptable to the particularistic South to hold all of it loyal to him except the nullifiers, and his strict construction attitude toward the Bank led both South and West to join hands in his support. For the support of New York he was largely indebted to Van Buren and his excellent political organization, the Albany Regency, which in combination with the Richmond Junto formed so effective an element in Jackson's support.

That it was not merely a victory for Jackson's character and personality but rather for the principles upon which he had stood was conclusively demonstrated by the complexion of the House of Representatives elected with him. So far was the Bank from achieving its needed two-thirds majority, that of the 240 members of this new body 140 were administration supporters.[89] Such being the case, it was entirely natural that Jackson should regard the result of the campaign in general as a vindication of his constitutional principles and of his policies, and in particular as a verdict against the Bank[90] which, aided by the National Republicans, had challenged him to a test of strength before the country.

[87] Ibid.
[88] Stanwood, History of Presidential Elections, p. 111.
[89] Niles' Register, vol. xlv, p. 228.
[90] Van Buren, Autobiography, p. 657.

APPENDIX I

PARTY NOMENCLATURE

To determine exactly when the terms "Democratic" and "Democratic Republican," on the one hand, and the term "National Republican," on the other, came to be applied to the followers of Jackson and to those of Adams and Clay respectively, is difficult. This cannot be categorically determined since usage varied in different States. Indeed the only sweeping statement applicable is that there never was any uniformity or consistency generally displayed by either party in its self-designation down to 1830; even as late as 1832 the Jacksonians referred to themselves officially as the "Republican party."[1]

The chief causes for the slow development of distinctive party names were: first, the reluctance of the various factions into which the old Republican party was split by the campaign of 1824 to regard themselves, or even to seem to appear, as other than the true Republican party; second, the fact that the campaigns of 1824 and 1828 were so largely based upon the personalities of the candidates instead of upon their political principles. Thus during the campaign of 1824 the Adams, Clay, Calhoun, Crawford and Jackson factions respectively considered themselves as parts of the old Republican party as it had existed under Madison and Monroe.

Party nomenclature began to take distinctive shape, locally at least, during the campaign of 1824. At the beginning of that contest the one party name in existence was "Republican." Indeed the party had been mostly so styled since

---

[1] See "Proceedings of a Convention of Republican Delegates . . . held at Baltimore, . . . May, 1832," History Pamphlets, vol. 293, Johns Hopkins University Library.

1812, as is shown by Jefferson's letters and by Niles' Register.[2] As the Adams and Clay factions inclined more toward each other in their advocacy of a nationalistic policy as to internal improvements, and still considered themselves and were considered within the Republican party, the descriptive adjective " national " began to be applied to them to differentiate them from the rather more particularistic followers of Jackson and Crawford. As far as can be ascertained the term " National Republican " was first applied to the Adams-Clay followers in New York during the latter stages of the campaign of 1824 when they united in the state legislature in order to defeat the Regency's effort to choose Crawford electors. Van Buren speaks of it thus: " The ' high minded ' [a little group of anti-Clintonian Federalists] espoused the cause of Mr. Adams zealously, and the feelings produced, or rather revived, by that contest carried them back into the federal ranks—then called National Republicans—where the survivors are still [1854] serving as Whigs." [3]   However this may have been, the term was not at all used in contemporary newspapers and letters.

In New York politics the name " Democratic " was also revived just prior to the opening of the national campaign of 1824. In 1818 there had been a split in the Republican party in the State, Clinton leading one faction and Van Buren the other.[4] The latter was dubbed by its enemies the " Bucktails," and about the same time began to refer to itself as the " Democratic " party.[5] The term " Republican," however, was still used to indicate both " Bucktails " and Clintonians.[6] As the Albany Regency under Van Buren's direction grew in strength and its party in the State became dominant, the term " Democratic " came to mean the Regency's party.

---

[2] Cf. Niles' Register, vols. i, ii, iii, ix, xi, xvii, xxi.

[3] Van Buren Autobiography, p. 108.

[4] Weed, Autobiography, p. 67.

[5] Van Buren, Autobiography, p. 98; Weed, p. 78; Hammond, vol. ii, pp. 86–87, 115, 139.

[6] Hammond, p. 139.

In Pennsylvania down to 1823 the general party term was "Republican" as distinguished from "Federalist." As the democracy of the State became more and more militant in its support of Jackson, the popular meetings of his followers all over the State used the term "Democrats" to describe themselves and their political principles and referred to the political body in which they claimed membership as the "democratic republican party."[7] The state convention which nominated Jackson for president was composed of delegates appointed by the "democratic republicans of this state."[8] At the same time however the convention referred to the congressional caucus as being made up of a "*minority* of the republican members of Congress*" and its action as being therefore a departure from "republican party" established usage.[9] This indicates that the party at large in the country was still styled the "Republican" and that Jackson's Pennsylvania supporters considered themselves as part of it.

So far as any generalization is possible from the above and other instances, it appears that both general groups— the followers of Crawford and Jackson on the one hand, and those of Adams and Clay on the other— into which the old Republican party was showing a tendency to divide by the end of 1823, still regarded themselves as Republicans and within the party thus designated. The terms "Democratic," "Democratic Republican" and "National Republican" had come into being as party names, but their use was confined to localities, States at most. The use of the first of these seems to have been confined to the Regency party in New York, that of the second to the Jacksonians in Pennsylvania, while the third was a designation for the Adams-Clay faction in New York plus the remnant of Federalists who joined them. Certainly there was no general use of any party name except "Republican."

---

[7] Niles' Register, vol. xxv, pp. 167, 195, 242–243; pamphlet in A. J. Donelson MSS. containing account of Jackson meeting at Pittsburg. Pa., November 14, 1823.

[8] Niles' Register, vol. xxvi, pp. 19–20.

[9] Ibid., p. 20.

Throughout the campaign of 1828 the same characteristics were manifested. The elimination of Crawford, the relegation of Calhoun and Clay to places of secondary importance, the election of Adams, and the union between his and Clay's followers operated to draw the line more sharply between the two opposing factions into which the shattered old Republican party had coalesced by the end of 1825. No other party name than " Republican," however, was generally used by either faction and each considered itself the true Republican party, the direct lineal descendant of that of Madison and Monroe.[10]   There is no evidence that either faction regarded its opponent as other than a schismatic Republican group ; indeed all the evidence points to this as the case. Clay stated this point of view exactly in a letter to Webster near the close of 1826 as follows : " We really have in this country no other than a Republican party. Names may be gotten up or kept up in particular states for local or personal purposes, but at this time there are but two parties in the Union, that of the administration and the opposition." [11]

In local practice throughout the country the use of party nomenclature was still inconsistent and varied. The single definite fact and also the only definite distinction in the use of names, as is shown in contemporary newspapers, was the nation-wide use of " the administration party " and " the opposition party," [12] or " the friends of General Jackson " and " the friends of the administration." [13]   Conventions were spoken of as " Adams " and " Jackson " conventions ; [14] a voter was an " Adams man " or a " Jackson man " ; [15] and the tickets nominated for state and local offices were known as " the Adams ticket " and " the Jackson ticket," the individual

[10] Ibid., vol. xxxi, p. 82.

[11] Clay to Webster, November 10, 1826, Webster MSS.

[12] Niles' Register, vol. xxx, p. 335.

[13] Baltimore Gazette, January 15, April 18, 1826, May 7, July 23, 1827 ; Baltimore American, May 23, 24, 1827 ; Niles' Register, vol. xxxi, p. 82.

[14] Niles' Register, vol. xxxiii, pp. 129–357, passim.

[15] Ibid., pp. 81, 333.

candidate being the "Adams candidate" or the "Jackson candidate."[16]

Aside from these terms based on the persons rather than upon their principles, there was no consistency or uniformity as to party designation. The Jackson paper in New Hampshire still referred to the supporters of the two parties as "Republicans" and "Federalists."[17] The Albany Argus spoke of "devotion to the republican cause and the interests of the democratic party" in the same sentence and connection.[18] After Jackson and Calhoun had become the party candidates, the Argus and the United States Telegraph each headed a column daily with "Republican National Ticket" over the names of the two men.[19] The Richmond Enquirer used the term "Republican" to refer to the Jackson party where the reference was unmistakable, but where it was not clear, used the conventional "Adams" or "Jackson" to distinguish.[20]

Only in Pennsylvania was there a definite drift toward the use of "Democratic" as a distinctive term. The term "democratic republican" had been used to describe the Jacksonians from the time the State began to stampede to him in 1823.[21] Hence "democratic republican" continued as the term mainly used in the campaign of 1828. Notwithstanding this there was a tendency to use "democratic" alone as the party designation. This tendency is illustrated by the references to the state convention at Harrisburg which was referred to by the party papers as the "Democratic Convention at Harrisburg."[22] It appears also in the convention's

---

[16] Ibid., p. 384.

[17] New Hampshire Patriot, quoted in Albany Argus, March 27, 1827.

[18] Albany Argus, September 7, 1827.

[19] See files of Argus and Telegraph during September and October, 1828.

[20] Richmond Enquirer, January 17, 1828.

[21] Pamphlet issued by Jackson meeting at Pittsburg, Pennsylvania, dated November 14, 1823, Donelson MSS.

[22] Pennsylvania Reporter, January 11, 1828; Telegraph, January 17, 1828.

nomination of Jackson " as the democratic candidate of Pennsylvania " for president.[23]

As to the Adams party, if Van Buren's memory was correct after twenty-five years, the name " National Republican " had been in existence since the campaign of 1824,[24] but there was certainly no general, and apparently no local, use of it during the campaign of 1828. As has been said the party was generally referred to among its friends as the " Republican " party if the reference was unmistakable, otherwise as the " friends of the administration " or " friends of Adams."

During the campaign of 1832, the use of party names rested more on party principles, hence for the most part the names of Jackson and Clay were discarded as descriptive adjectives. As nearly as can be determined, the name " National Republican" became current during the year 1830, about the time that party launched Clay's campaign.[25] Niles begins using it and it begins to appear in letters about the end of 1830 and the beginning of 1831.[26] In the first two months of 1831 it became fixed party usage. During the process of effecting the party's organization in New York City it was used exclusively;[27] it was also used for the most part by the state conventions held in Connecticut and Maine at this time.[28]

" National Republican " received what may be called the final stamp of approval as the party's official title by the National Intelligencer in its issue of February 22, 1831, thus: " *National Republican* is an excellent designation for a national party in our republican Union. Let it be adopted everywhere, by all who would uphold the Federal Constitution; secure the independence and continuance of the Su-

[23] Telegraph, Jan. 17, 1828; Pennsylvania Reporter, Jan. 17, 1828.
[24] Van Buren, Autobiography, p. 108.
[25] Seward, Autobiography, pp. 74, 76.
[26] Cf. Niles' Register, vol. xxxix, p. 330; P. P. F. Degrand to Biddle, January 23, 1831, Biddle MSS.
[27] National Intelligencer, January 4, February 17, 1831.
[28] Ibid., February 24, March 7, 1831.

preme Court; preserve a sound currency; possess a substantive and enlightened President of the United States; prevent offices from becoming the booty of mere partisans and parasites; and obtain a truly responsible and visible government." [29] Hence it is to be expected, and this was actually the case, that the proceedings of the party's two conventions, that at Baltimore in December, 1831, and that at Washington the following May, should be printed by order of those bodies under the respective titles of "Journal of the National Republican Convention" and "Proceedings of the National Republican Convention of Young Men." [30]

During the campaign the use of "Democratic" as a designation for the party increased somewhat in favor with the Jacksonians but did not by any means displace "Republican" as the party's official title. "Democratic Republican" was, however, the most frequently used of the three names, no doubt in order to differentiate the party more sharply from the National Republican. Seward states that "The campaign for 1832 opened with the year 1830. The Republican party, now taking to itself the more radical name of 'the Democratic party,' announced . . . its determination to secure the reelection of Andrew Jackson." [31] Seward's memory here seems at fault since the New York Courier and Enquirer, then staunchly Jacksonian, in the same article referred to the Jackson party by all three names, as "republican party," "democratic party" and "democratic republicans." [32]

In Pennsylvania "Democratic Republican" remained the most prevalent term, with "Democratic" used to some extent,[33] and this seems to have been the case in New Hamp-

---

[29] Ibid., February 22, 1831.
[30] History Pamphlets, vol. 293, Nos. 17, 18, Johns Hopkins University Library.
[31] Seward, Autobiography, p. 76.
[32] New York Courier and Enquirer, March 12, 1830, in Niles' Register, vol. xxxviii, p. 110.
[33] Cf. Niles' Register, vol. xxxvi, p. 134; vol. xl, p. 61; vol. xlii, p. 72.

shire also.[34] A letter from Richards to McLean shows that the Jackson ticket in Philadelphia " is called simply the Democratic ticket." [35] For all these local variations, and the probable increased use of " Democratic Republican," [36] the official designation of the party remained " Republican." Thus The Globe, the Albany Argus, and the Richmond Enquirer usually referred to their party by the latter name, and Jackson, Kendall and other leaders so designated it in their letters.[37] This official title of the party conclusively appears in the caption of the proceedings of its convention in Baltimore, as " A Convention of Republican Delegates." [38]

To generalize categorically concerning this usage, which was so varied and which crystallized so gradually, is venturesome. The following facts, however, seem to stand out with some degree of clearness. As to the designation of the followers of Adams and, later, of Clay, the term " National Republican " may have been coined as early as the campaign of 1824, according to Van Buren,[39] or in that of 1828, according to Seward,[40] but the name certainly did not attain general or official usage before 1830, after Clay's campaign was under way. As to the Jackson party, the designations "Democratic" and "Democratic Republican" were both used in the campaign of 1824,[41] but in a few localities only. The party, like that of Adams and Clay, still regarded itself as the Republican party, and this name continued as the official one to the close of the campaign of 1832, with " Democratic Republican " gaining but not supplanting " Republican " in current usage.

---

[34] Ibid., vol. xxxviii, p. 332.
[35] Richards to McLean, October 1, 1831, McLean MSS.
[36] Globe, May 1, 1832.
[37] Kendall to A. G. Meriweather, May 22, 1829, Jackson to Tammany Society, May 2, 1831, quoted in Niles' Register, vol. xxxvi, p. 241; vol. xl, p. 229.
[38] History Pamphlets, vol. 293, No. 22, Johns Hopkins University Library.
[39] Van Buren, Autobiography, p. 108.
[40] Seward, Autobiography, p. 64.
[41] Van Buren, Autobiography, p. 98; pamphlet dated November 14, 1823, in Donelson MSS.

APPENDIX II

Van Buren's Letter to the Shocco Springs, N. C., Committee

Owasco, Cayuga County, [New York,]
October 4, 1832.

Gentlemen: Your letter of the 25th August found me at this place. I regret extremely that the delay in its reception, occasioned by my absence, has prevented an earlier attention to its contents.

By the resolutions which you have been appointed to communicate to me, I am advised that those by whom they were adopted, desire to be informed of my sentiments "on the subjects of the protective system and its proper adjustment, internal improvement, the Bank of the United States, and nullification."

The right of those you represent, to be informed of my opinions on those interesting subjects, as derived from the position in which the favor of my fellow citizens has placed me, is undoubted; and in cheerfully complying with their request, I have only to regret, that the inconvenience of the situation in which it finds me, consequent upon the hurry and confusion attending the further prosecution of my journey, and the importance, to the fulfilment of the objects of your constituents, of as little delay as possible in the transmission of the communication, preclude anything like an elaborate discussion of the subjects under consideration, if indeed such a course would, under more favorable circumstances, be desirable to you. The regret, however, which I might otherwise experience on this account, is relieved by the hope, that my fellow citizens of North Carolina, preferring, with characteristic good sense, results to speculations, will be as well satisfied, and as effectually aided in the intelligent bestowment of their suffrages, by a brief but explicit avowal of my opinions, as they would be by an elaborate dissertation upon subjects which have been so thoroughly and diffusively debated.

Although my official acts in relation to the protective system, might well be regarded as rendering the avowal unnecessary, I think it, nevertheless, proper to say, that I believe the establishment of commercial regulations, with a view to the encouragement of domestic products, to be within the constitutional power of Congress. Whilst, however, I have entertained this opinion, it has never been my wish to see the power in question exercised with an oppressive inequality upon any portion of our citizens, or for the advantage of one section of the union at the expense of another. On the contrary, I have at all times believed it to be the sacred duty of those who are entrusted with the administration of the federal government, to direct its operations in the manner best calculated to distribute as equally as possible its burthens and blessings amongst the several states and the people. My views upon this subject were several years ago spread before the people of this state, and have since been widely diffused through the medium of the public press. My object at that time was to invite the attention of my immediate constituents to a dispassionate consideration of the subject in its various bearings; being well assured, that such an investigation would bring them to a standard, which, from its moderation and justice, would furnish the best guarantee for the true interests of all. If, as has been supposed, those views have contributed in any degree to produce a state of feeling so much to be desired, I have reason to be gratified with the result.

The approaching, and if the policy of the present Executive is allowed to prevail, the certain and speedy extinguishment of the national debt, has presented an opportunity for a more equitable adjustment of the tariff, which has already been embraced by the adoption of a conciliatory measure, the spirit of which will, I doubt not, continue to be cherished by all who are not desirous of advancing their private interests at the sacrifice of those of the public, and who place a just value upon the peace and harmony of the union.

The protective system and its proper adjustment, became a subject of frequent and necessary consideration, whilst I formed a part of the cabinet; and the manner in which the president proposed to carry into effect the policy in relation to imposts, recommended in his previous messages, has since been avowed with that frankness which belongs to his character. To this end he recommended " a modification of the tariff, which should produce a reduction of the revenue to the wants of the government, and an adjustment of the duty upon imports, with a view to equal justice in relation to all our national interests, and to the counteraction of foreign policy, so far as it may be injurious to those interests." [1]

In these sentiments I fully concur; and I have been thus explicit in my statement of them, that there may be no room for misapprehension as to my own views upon the subject. A sincere and faithful application of these principles to our legislation, unwarped by private interest or political design; a restriction of the wants of the government to a simple and economical administration of its affairs—the only administration which is consistent with the purity and stability of the republican system;—a preference in encouragement given, to such manufactures as are essential to the national defence, and its extension to others in proportion as they are adapted to our country, and of which the raw material is produced by ourselves; with a proper respect for the rule that demands that all taxes should be imposed in proportion to the ability and condition of the contributors;—would, I am convinced, give ultimate satisfaction to a vast majority of the people of the United States, and arrest that spirit of discontent which is now unhappily so prevalent, and which threatens such extensive injury to the institutions of our country.

Internal improvements are so diversified in their nature, and the possible agency of the federal government in their construction, so

---

[1] Quoted by Van Buren from Jackson's third annual message; cf. Richardson, Messages and Papers, vol. ii, p. 556.

variable in its character and degree, as to render it not a little difficult to lay down any precise rule that will embrace the whole subject. The broadest and best defined division, is that which distinguishes between the direct construction of works of internal improvement by the general government, and pecuniary assistance given by it to such as are undertaken by others. In the former, are included the right to make and establish roads and canals within the states, and the assumption of as much jurisdiction over the territory they occupy, as is necessary to their preservation and use: the latter is restricted to simple grants of money, in aid of such works, when made under state authority.

The federal government does not, in my opinion, possess the first power specified; nor can it derive it from the assent of the state in which such works are to be constructed. The money power, as it is called, is not so free from difficulty. Various rules have from time to time been suggested by those who properly appreciate the importance of precision and certainty in the operations of the federal power; but they have been so frequently infringed upon by the apparently unavoidable action of the government, that a final and satisfactory settlement of the questions has been prevented. The wide difference between the definition of the power in question upon paper, and its practical application to the operations of government, has been sensibly felt by all who have been entrusted with the management of the public affairs. The whole subject was reviewed in the president's Maysville message. Sincerely believing that the best interests of the whole country, the quiet, not to say stability, of the union, and the preservation of that moral force which perhaps as much as any other holds it together, imperiously required that the destructive force of legislation upon that subject, then prevalent, should, in some proper and constitutional way, be arrested, I throughout gave to the measure of which that document was an exposition, my active, zealous and anxious support.

The opinions declared by the president in the Maysville, and his succeeding annual message, as I understand them, are as follows: 1st. That Congress does not possess the power to make and establish a road or canal within a state, with the right of jurisdiction to the extent I have stated; and that if it is the wish of the people that the construction of such works should be undertaken by the federal government, a previous amendment of the constitution conferring that power, and defining and restricting its exercise, with reference to the sovereignty of the states, is indispensable. 2d. An intimation of his belief that the right to make appropriations in aid of such internal improvements as are of a national character, has been so generally acted upon, and so long acquiesced in by the federal and state governments, and the constituents of each, as to justify its exercise; but, that it is nevertheless highly expedient that even such appropriations should, with the exception of such as relate to lighthouses, beacons, buoys, piers and other improvements, in the harbors and navigable rivers of the United States, for the security and facility of our foreign commerce, be deferred at least until the national debt is paid. 3d. That if it is the wish of the people that the agency of the federal government should be restricted to the appropriation of money, and extended in that form, in aid of such undertakings, when carried on by state authority, then the occasion, the manner and extent of the appropriation, should be made the subject of constitutional regulation.

In these views I concurred; and I likewise participated in the difficulties which were encountered, and expressed by the president, in adopting the principle which concedes to the federal government the right to make appropriations in aid of works which might be regarded as of a national character—difficulties which arose as well from the danger of considering mere usage the foundation of the right, as from the extreme uncertainty and consequent insecurity of the best rule that had ever been adopted, or that could, in the absence of a positive constitutional provision, be established. The reasons on which these objections were founded, are so fully stated in the document referred to, and have been so extensively promulgated that it is unnecessary for me to repeat them here. Subsequent reflection and experience have confirmed my apprehensions of the injurious consequences which would probably flow from the usurpation of appropriations for internal improvements, with no better rule for the government of congress than that of which I have spoken; and I do not hesitate to express it as my opinion, that the general and true interests of the country would be best consulted by withholding them, with the exceptions which I have already referred to, until some constitutional regulation upon the subject has been made.

In this avowal, I am certainly not influenced by feelings of indifference, much less of hostility, to internal improvements. As such they can have no enemies. I have never omitted to give them all the proper aid in my power; for which, by the way, I claim no particular merit, as I do not believe there is an honest and sane man in the country who does not wish to see them prosper: but their construction, and the manner in which and the means by which they are to be affected, are quite different questions. Rather than again expose our legislation to all the corrupting influences of those scrambles and combinations in congress, which have been heretofore witnessed, and the other affairs of the country to the injurious effects unavoidably resulting from them, it would, in my opinion, be infinitely preferable to leave works of the character spoken of, and not embraced in the exception which has been pointed out, for the present, to the supports upon which they have reposed with so much success for the last two years, viz: state efforts and private enterprise. If the great body of the people become convinced that the progress of these works should be accelerated by the federal arm, they will not refuse to come to some proper constitutional arrangement upon the subject. The supposition that an equitable rule, which pays a proper respect to the interests and condition of the different states, could fail to receive, ultimately, the constitutional sanction, would be doing injustice to the intelligence of the country. By such a settlement of the question, our political system, in addition to the other advantages derived from it, would, in relation to this subject at least, be relieved from those dangerous shocks which spring from diversities of opinion upon constitutional points of deep interest; and, in the meantime, the resources of the country would be best husbanded by being left in the hands of those by whose labor they are produced.

I am unreservedly opposed to the renewal of the charter of the United States bank, and approve of the refusal of the president to sign the bill, passed for that purpose, at the last session of congress, as well on account of the unconstitutionality, as the impolicy of its provisions.

I am equally opposed to the principle of nullification, as it is called. With whatever sincerity that doctrine may be entertained by others, I believe that it is entirely destitute of constitutional authority, and that it could not be adopted, without drawing after it the ultimate but certain destruction of the confederacy.

That these views will be universally acceptable to those who have called them forth, I do not allow myself to expect. He who thinks in a country, the interests of which are so diversified as ours, and in respect to the constitution of which construction is made to perform so great a part, that the purest intentions, or the most profound reflections, can enable him so to shape his political tenets as to meet the approbation of all; or who is so unreasonable as to require that those of the public service should, in all respects, correspond with his own, must expect to make up his account with disappointment or deception. For myself, I cherish no such hope. All I ask, is a fair confidence in the sincerity of the principles I have avowed, and in the fidelity with which they will be maintained. It is not possible that any nomination could have been more entirely unsolicited, by word or deed, than that which has been bestowed upon me. Had it not been for the event to which, as I have before said, I feel myself principally indebted for it, I should not have hesitated to decline, however highly distinguished the honor intended for me is felt to be. And I beg my fellow citizens of North Carolina to believe, that, notwithstanding the deep sense which, in common with the people of the union, I entertain of their unwavering though unpretending patriotism and unspotted political faith, and the high gratification I should derive from being thought worthy of their confidence, I shall feel it a duty to be content with whatever disposition of the question they, in the honest exercise of their opinions, shall see fit to make.

With sentiments of high consideration, I am, gentlemen, your obedient servant,

M. VAN BUREN.

To *Joseph H. Bryan, Josiah T. Granberry* and *Memucan Hunt, esqs.*, committee, &c.

This letter in pamphlet form is in the Van Buren MSS.

APPENDIX III

THE FIRST POLITICAL PARTY PLATFORM

Adopted by the National Republican Convention of young men on May 10, 1832. This convention met at Washington, D. C., May 7–12, 1832.

On motion of Mr. Flagg, of South Carolina, seconded by Mr. Perkins, of Connecticut, it was

Resolved, That a committee, consisting of one individual from each State represented in this Convention, and the District of Columbia, be appointed to draft resolutions upon such subjects as shall be deemed proper to be acted upon by this Convention.

The following gentlemen were accordingly selected for this purpose:

Messrs. William Paine, of Maine; E. Seymour, of Vermont; T. Darling, of New Hampshire; Thomas Kinnicutt, of Massachusetts; James Anthony, of Rhode Island; C. M. Emerson, of Connecticut; C. Morgan, jun., of New York; J. D. Miller, of New Jersey; E. T. McDowell, of Pennsylvania; Evan H. Thomas, of Delaware; Thomas G. Pratt, of Maryland; Andrew Hunter, of Virginia; Henry C. Flagg, of South Carolina; S. Brown, of Louisiana; William N. Bullitt, of Kentucky; Edward H. Cumming, of Ohio; Thomas P. Coleman, of the District of Columbia.

. . . .

Mr. Kinnicutt, of Massachusetts, from the Committee on Resolutions, reported the following:

1. *Resolved,* That, in the opinion of this Convention, although the fundamental principles adopted by our fathers, as a basis upon which to rear the superstructure of American independence, can never be annihilated, yet the time has come when nothing short of the united energies of all the friends of the American Republic can be relied on, to sustain and perpetuate that hallowed work.

2. *Resolved,* That an adequate protection to American industry is indispensable to the prosperity of the country; and that an abandonment of the policy at this period would be attended with consequences ruinous to the best interests of the nation.

3. *Resolved,* That a uniform system of internal improvements sustained and supported by the General Government, is calculated to secure, in the highest degree, the harmony, the strength, and the permanency of the Republic.

4. *Resolved,* That the Supreme Court of the United States is the only tribunal recognized by the constitution for deciding, in the last resort, all questions arising under the constitution and laws of the United States, and that, upon the preservation of the authority and jurisdiction of that court inviolate, depends the existence of the Union.

5. *Resolved,* That the Senate of the United States is preeminently a conservative branch of the Federal Government; that, upon a fearless and independent exercise of its constitutional functions, depends the existence of the nicely balanced powers of that Government; and that all attempts to overawe its deliberations, by the public press, or by the national Executive, deserve the indignant reprobation of every American citizen.

6. *Resolved,* That the political course of the present Executive has given us no pledge that he will defend and support these great principles of American policy and of the constitution; but, on the contrary, has convinced us that he will abandon them whenever the purposes of party require.

7. *Resolved,* That the indiscriminate removal of public officers, for a mere difference of political opinion, is a gross abuse of power; and that the doctrine lately "boldly preached" in the Senate of the United States, that to the "victor belong the spoils of the enemy," is detrimental to the interests, corrupting to the morals, and dangerous to the liberties of the People of this country.

8. *Resolved,* That we hold the disposition shown by the present national administration, to accept the advice of the King of Holland, touching the northeastern boundary line of the United States, and thus to transfer a portion of the territory and citizens of a State of this Union to a foreign power, to manifest a total destitution of patriotic American feeling; in as much as we consider the life, liberty, property, and citizenship of every inhabitant of every State, as entitled to the national protection.

9. *Resolved,* That the arrangement between the United States and Great Britain relative to the colonial trade, made in pursuance of the instructions of the late Secretary of State was procured in a manner derogatory to the national character, and is injurious to this country in its practical results.

10. *Resolved,* That it is the duty of every citizen of this Republic, who regards the honor, the prosperity, and the preservation of our Union, to oppose, by every honorable measure, the re-election of ANDREW JACKSON, and to promote the election of HENRY CLAY, of Kentucky, and JOHN SERGEANT, of Pennsylvania, as President and Vice President of the United States.[1]

---

[1] From "Proceedings of the National Republican Convention of Young Men, which assembled in the City of Washington, May 7, 1832." Printed, Gales and Seaton, Washington, 1832. In History Pamphlets, vol. 293, No. 18, Johns Hopkins University Library.

THE POPULAR VOTE IN 1832 [1]

State	Jackson	Clay	Wirt	Approximate majority or plurality
Maine........	33,984	27,362	841	Jackson over both.........5,781
New Hampshire	25,146	19,454	..,...[b]	Jackson over Clay......... 5,692
Vermont......	7,870	11,152	13,106	Wirt's plurality. 1,954
Massachusetts .	13,933	32,006	14,692	Clay over both. 3,381
Rhode Island..	1,000[a]	2,000[a]	500[a]	Clay over both. 500
Connecticut....	11,041	17,518	3,335	Clay over both. 3,142
New York[2]....	168,243	154,896		Jackson over both.........13,347
New Jersey....	23,826	23,466	468	Jackson's plurality.......... 360
Pennsylvania ..	90,983	..,...[b]	66,716	Jackson over Wirt.........24,267
Delaware......	4,105	4,276	..,...[b]	Clay over Jackson.......... 171
Maryland.....	19,199	19,150	..,...[b]	Jackson over Clay......... 49
Virginia.......	33,649	11,582	..,...[b]	Jackson over Clay.........22,067
North Carolina	24,385	4,563	..,...[b]	Jackson over Clay.........19,822
South Carolina	{ Electors chosen by legislature and voted for John Floyd of Virginia.			
Georgia.......	30,000[a]	..,...[b]	..,...[b]	Jackson.........30,000
Alabama......	10,000[a]	3,000[a]	..,...[b]	Jackson over Clay......... 7,000
Mississippi.....	2,000[a]	800[a]	..,...[b]	Jackson over Clay......... 1,200
Louisiana......	3,546	1,954	..,...[b]	Jackson over Clay......... 1,592
Tennessee.....	40,000[a]	2,000[a]	..,...[b]	Jackson over Clay.........38,000
Kentucky.....	13,000[a]	27,000[a]	..,...[b]	Clay over Jackson..........14,000
Ohio..........	81,246	76,539	509	Jackson over both......... 4,198
Indiana.......	13,000[a]	11,000[a]	..,...[b]	Jackson over Clay......... 2,000
Illinois........	5,000[a]	3,000[a]	..,...[b]	Jackson over Clay......... 2,000
Missouri.......	6,000[a]	2,000[a]	..,...[b]	Jackson over Clay......... 4,000
Total.....	661,156	454,718	100,167	

[1] The above figures and estimates are based chiefly on Niles' Register, vol. xliii, pp. 135–251 passim.

[2] Antimasonic vote in New York is combined with the National Republican, as the two parties chose the same ticket of electors.

[a] Estimate of vote.

[b] No ticket in the field.

BIBLIOGRAPHY

Sources

Manuscripts

The Papers of Nicholas Biddle.
The Papers of Andrew Jackson Donelson.
The Papers of Andrew Jackson.
The Papers of John McLean.
The Papers of Andrew Stevenson.
The Papers of Nicholas P. Trist.
The Papers of Martin Van Buren.
The Papers of Daniel Webster.

(The above are in the Manuscript Division of the
Library of Congress)

Autobiographies, Memoirs, Published Letters and Contemporary Accounts

Adams, John Quincy, Memoirs, comprising portions of his diary from 1795 to 1848. Charles Francis Adams, Editor. 12 vols. J. B. Lippincott & Co., Philadelphia, 1874.
—— Writings. Worthington C. Ford, Editor. 7 vols. The Macmillan Co., New York, 1913-.
Barnes, Thurlow Weed, A Memoir of Thurlow Weed. Houghton, Mifflin & Co., Boston, 1884.
Benton, Thomas Hart, Abridgment of the Debates of Congress from 1789 to 1856. 16 vols. D. Appleton & Co., New York, 1859.
—— Thirty Years' View . . . from 1820 to 1850. 2 vols. D. Appleton & Co., New York, 1854.
Calhoun, John C., Correspondence. J. F. Jameson, Editor. The Annual Report of the American Historical Association for the Year 1899, vol. ii.
Clay, Henry, Life and Speeches. Daniel Mallory, Editor. 2 vols. Greeley & M'Elrath, New York, 1844.
—— Private Correspondence. Calvin Colton, Editor. Frederick Parker, Boston, 1856.
Hamilton, James A., Reminiscences, or Men and Events at Home and Abroad during Three-quarters of a Century. Charles Scribner & Sons, New York, 1869.
Hammond, Jabez D., History of Political Parties in the State of New York. 3 vols. H. E. Finney, Cooperstown, 1844.
Jefferson, Thomas, Writings. Paul L. Ford, Editor. 10 vols. G. P. Putnam's Sons, New York, 1893–1899.
Kendall, Amos, Autobiography. William Stickney, Editor. Lee & Shepard, Boston, 1872.

Sargent, Nathan, Public Men and Events from Monroe's Adminis-
tration in 1817 to the Close of Fillmore's in 1852. 2 vols. J.
B. Lippincott & Co., Philadelphia, 1875.
Scott, Nancy N., Memoir of Hugh Lawson White, with selections
from his Speeches and Correspondence. J. B. Lippincott & Co.,
Philadelphia, 1856.
Seward, William H., Autobiography from 1801 to 1834. Frederick
W. Seward, Editor. D. Appleton & Co., New York, 1891.
Smith, Mrs. Samuel H., The First Forty Years of Washington So-
ciety. Gaillard Hunt, Editor. Charles Scribner's Sons, New
York, 1906.
Van Buren, Martin, Autobiography. John C. Fitzpatrick, Editor.
The Annual Report of the American Historical Association for
the Year 1918, vol. ii.
Webster, Daniel, Private Correspondence. Fletcher Webster,
Editor. 2 vols. Little, Brown & Co., Boston, 1857.
Weed, Thurlow, Autobiography. Harriet A. Weed, Editor. Hough-
ton, Mifflin & Co., Boston, 1884.

Public Documents

American State Papers, Foreign Relations, vol. v. Gales & Seaton,
Washington, 1858.
Annals of the Congress of the United States, 18th Congress, 1st
Session, vol. i. Gales & Seaton, Washington, 1856.
Messages and Papers of the Presidents, vol. ii. James D. Richard-
son, Compiler. Government Printing Office, 1896.
Public Statutes at Large of the United States of America, vol. iii.
Little & Brown, Boston, 1848.
Congressional Debates, vol. viii, part 1, 22nd Congress, 1st Session.
Gales & Seaton, Washington, 1833.
House Report, No. 460, 22nd Congress, 1st Session.
Senate Journal, 22nd Congress, 1st Session.
Senate Document No. 17, 23rd Congress, 2nd Session.

Newspapers

(Files of these papers in Library of Congress unless
otherwise noted)

The Albany Argus.
The Baltimore American. Library of the Maryland Historical So-
ciety, Balto.
The Baltimore Gazette. Library of the Maryland Historical So-
ciety, Balto.
The Daily Globe. [Washington].
The Marylander. [Baltimore]. Library of the Maryland Historical
Society, Balto.
The Morning Courier and Enquirer. [New York].
The National Gazette. [Philadelphia].
The National Intelligencer. [Washington].
Niles' Weekly Register. [Baltimore].
The Pennsylvania Reporter and Democratic Herald. [Harrisburg].
The Richmond Enquirer.
The United States Telegraph. [Washington].

Pamphlets

The Anti-Masonic Review, I, II. In collection of Antimasonic
Pamphlets of the Maryland Historical Society.
" Proceedings of a Convention of Delegates from the different
counties in the State of New York opposed to Free-Masonry.
Held . . . in the City of Albany on the 19, 20, and 21st day of
February, 1829." Antimasonic Pamphlets of Maryland Historical Society.
" The Proceedings of the United States Antimasonic Convention
held at Philadelphia, September 11, 1830, embracing the Journal
of Proceedings, the Reports, the Debates and the Address to
the People." Antimasonic Pamphlets of the Maryland Historical Society.
" Proceedings of the Second United States Antimasonic Convention,
held at Baltimore, September, 1831, Journal and Reports, nominations of candidates for President and Vice President of the
United States, Letters of Acceptance, Resolutions and Address
to the People." Antimasonic Pamphlets of the Maryland Historical Society.
" Journal of the National Republican Convention, which assembled
in the City of Baltimore, Dec. 12, 1831. . . . Published by order
of the Convention." History Pamphlets, vol. 293, Johns Hopkins University Library.
" Proceedings of the National Convention of Young Men which
assembled in the City of Washington May 7, 1832." History
Pamphlets, vol. 293, Johns Hopkins University Library.
" Summary of the Proceedings of a Convention of Republican Delegates, for the several states in the Union, for the purpose of
nominating a candidate for the office of Vice President of the
United States; held at Baltimore, in the State of Maryland,
May, 1832." History Pamphlets, vol. 293, Johns Hopkins University Library.
Pamphlet issued by a " Democratic Republican Meeting " held " at
the court house in the City of Pittsburg on Friday evening,
November 14th, 1823," by citizens of Allegheny County " friendly
to the election of Andrew Jackson." In the Andrew J. Donelson Papers, Library of Congress.
Pamphlet " Letter from Martin Van Buren in reply to the letter
of a Committee appointed at a public meeting held at Shocco
Springs, North Carolina." In the Van Buren Papers, Library
of Congress.

SECONDARY WORKS

Adams, Henry, The Degradation of Democratic Dogma. Brooks
Adams, Ed. Macmillan, New York, 1919.
—— History of the United States . . . 1801–1816. 9 vols. Charles
Scribner's Sons, New York, 1891.
—— Life of Albert Gallatin. J. B. Lippincott & Co., Philadelphia,
1879.
Ambler, Charles H., Thomas Ritchie, a Study in Virginia Politics.
Bell Book & Stationery Co., Richmond, 1913.
Bassett, John Spencer, Life of Andrew Jackson. 2 vols. Double-
day, Page & Co., Garden City, New York, 1911.

Catterall, Ralph C. H., The Second Bank of the United States. University of Chicago Press, Chicago, 1903.

Channing, Edward, History of the United States, 1789–1815. 4 vols. Macmillan, New York, 1912–1917.

Houston, David F., A Critical Study of Nullification in South Carolina. Longmans, Green & Co., New York, 1896.

Hunt, Gaillard, John C. Calhoun. George W. Jacobs & Co., Philadelphia, 1908.

McCarthy, Charles, The Antimasonic Party; A Study of Political Antimasonry in the United States, 1827–1840. The Annual Report of the American Historical Association for the Year 1902, vol. i, Chap. XVI.

McMaster, John Bach, A History of the People of the United States from the Revolution to the Civil War. 8 vols. D. Appleton & Co., New York, 1884–1913.

Oberholtzer, Ellis P., Philadelphia, A History of the City and People. 4 vols. The S. J. Clarke Publishing Co., Philadelphia, 1912.

Parton, James, Life of Andrew Jackson. 3 vols. Mason Brothers, New York, 1860.

Scharf, J. Thomas, The Chronicles of Baltimore. Turnbull Brothers, Baltimore, 1874.

Stanwood, Edward, A History of Presidential Elections, 3rd ed. revised. Houghton, Mifflin & Co., Boston, 1892.

INDEX

Adams, John Quincy, initial political strength of, 13–14; elected President by House through Clay's support, 19; political effects on, of appointing Clay to State Department, 21; effect of his inaugural and first annual messages, 22–23; opposition to, forming, 23; overwhelming defeat in 1828, 30–31; approached by Antimasons in campaign of 1832, 44; rumors of Antimasonic nomination of, at Baltimore, 48.

Addresses, political, character of, and difference from platform, 140.

Albany Argus, mouthpiece of the Regency, edited by Crosswell, 12.

Albany Regency, character and power of, in New York, 12; loses control of the State, 18–19; regains control, 25–26; reallied with Junto, 25–26; effective support of Jackson in, 18–32, 154.

Alliance, first instance of, between South and West, 31; political, between Virginia and New York, 12, 20, 25–26.

Antimasonic Convention, used locally by the party from outset, 34; significance of, at Albany, 34–35; call for, at Philadelphia, 35–36; at Philadelphia, 38–42; probability of nomination of McLean by, at Baltimore, 44–45, 47–48; at Baltimore, 45–52; precedents established, 51–52.

Antimasonic party, origin of, 29; union with Adams' followers in New York causes split in, 30, 33; leaders of, desire to use movement for political ends, 33, 35–37, 40–41; elements comprising, 32; committee of, appointed at Utica, analogous to present party national committee, 34; significance for, of Albany convention, 34; holds first national party convention, 38–42; opposed to Jackson, 36; spreads rapidly in North, 37; Clay's attitude toward, 43; holds first national nominating convention, 45–52; Wirt's attitude toward, 49–51, 142–143; union with National Republicans in New York, 145–146; causes of defeat in 1832.

Bank, United States, Jackson's attitude toward, 105–106, 123–124; nature of, 106–108; efforts to secure Jackson's good will for, 109–110; effect of Jackson's first message on, 111; becomes identified with National Republican party, 118–119; expenditures for propaganda, 120–121, 150–151; McLane's report on, 121–123; National Republican party adopts, as chief issue, 125; applies for recharter, 128; congressional reports on, 133; the central campaign issue, 134; recharter of, vetoed, 134, 149.

Barber, James, 67, 70.

Barber, Philip, 49, 91, 144, 145.

Barry, William T., 75, 77, 89–90, 133.

Benton, Thomas H., on effect of internal improvements on campaign of 1824, 15; on rejection of Van Buren's nomination, 93; leads in fight against recharter, 118, 120, 133.

Berrien, J. McP., 73, 76, 77, 79, 89.

Bibliography, 171–174.

Biddle, Nicholas, president of the Bank, 105–106; clashes

work in Congress for re-
charter of Bank, 133; Clay's
gloomy letter to, over prospect
in Kentucky, 151–152.

Weed, Thurlow, 33, 34, 35, 37,
38, 47, 49, 50, 146.

Welles, Gideon, editor of Jackson paper, reveals Duff

Green's plot against Jackson's
leadership, 84.

Wirt, William, attitude toward
Antimasons, 49–51; letter to
McLean on political outlook,
142–143.

Woodbury, Levi, 90, 133.